A Medieval Life
Cecilia Penifader of Brigstock, c. 1295–1344

A Medieval Life

Cecilia Penifader of Brigstock, c. 1295-1344

Judith M. Bennett

McGraw-Hill College

Boston   Burr Ridge, IL   Dubuque, IA   Madison, WI   New York   San Francisco   St. Louis
Bangkok   Bogotá   Caracas   Lisbon   London   Madrid
Mexico City   Milan   New Delhi   Seoul   Singapore   Sydney   Taipei   Toronto

McGraw-Hill College

A Division of The McGraw·Hill Companies

A MEDIEVAL LIFE
CECILIA PENIFADER OF BRIGSTOCK, c. 1295-1344

This book is printed on acid-free paper.

2 3 4 5 6 7 8 9 0 DOC/DOC 9 3 2 1 0 9

ISBN 0-07-290331-7

Editorial director: *Jane E. Vaicunas*
Senior sponsoring editor: *Lyn Uhl*
Developmental editor: *Donata Dettbarn*
Senior marketing manager: *Suzanne Daghlian*
Senior project manager: *Marilyn Rothenberger*
Production supervisor: *Sandy Ludovissy*
Freelance design coordinator: *Mary L. Christianson*
Photo research coordinator: *John C. Leland*
Compositor: *Shepherd, Inc.*
Typeface: *10/12 Palatino*
Printer: *R. R. Donnelley & Sons Company/Crawfordsville/IN*

Freelance cover designer: *Elise Lansdon*
Cover image: © *Bibliotheque royale Albert I Bruxelles/folio 59/Brussells, KBR., 1175*

The credits section for this book begins on page 147 and is considered an extension of the copyright page.

Library of Congress Cataloging-in-Publication Data

Bennett, Judith M.
   A medieval life-Cecilia Penifader of Brigstock, c. 1295-1344 /
  Judith M. Bennett. - 1st ed.
cm.
   Includes index.
   ISBN 0-07-290331-7
Brigstock (England)-Biography. 2. Women-England-Brigstock-
  -History-Middle Ages, 500-1500. 3. England-Social
  conditions-1066-1485. 4. Penifader, Cecilia, ca. 1295-1344.
  5. Brigstock (England)-History. I. Title.
  DA690.B785B46   1999
  942.5'54-dc21   98-20580
  [b]   CIP

www.mhhe.com

Acknowledgments

I have benefited greatly from the generous assistance of many people, but I am especially grateful to Sandy Bardsley who gave me a timely reminder of my plans for a study of Cecilia Penifader. In her capacity as a research assistant, Sandy Bardsley responded to an avalanche of requests with enthusiasm and creativity, and as one of those who read the manuscript, she improved it in innumerable ways. Cynthia Herrup, Maryanne Kowaleski, Christopher Whittick, and Merry Wiesner also offered invaluable criticisms of drafts, and Glenn Foard, County Archaeological Officer for the Northamptonshire County Council, answered my many questions both promptly and patiently. I have not taken all of their advice, but *A Medieval Life* is much better for their efforts. Cynthia Herrup endured my fascination with the life and times of Cecilia Penifader with her customary good humor and grace. Leslye Jackson and Amy Mack offered invaluable editorial guidance. I am grateful to Rachel Watson, County Archivist of Northamptonshire, the Duke of Buccleuch KT, and Peter Moyse for their assistance in reproducing photographs of the Brigstock records.

The photographs taken from the Brigstock court rolls on pages 7 and 129 are reproduced with permission of the Duke of Buccleuch, KT. The roll shown on page 7 [item 4] is from the Northamptonshire Record Office, Box 364A, roll 26. The doodle shown on page 129 is taken from Northamptonshire Record Office, Box X365, roll 51. The drawing found on page 18 is derived from a reconstruction found in Maurice Beresford and John Hurst, *Wharram Percy: Deserted Medieval Village* (Yale University Press, 1991), p. 40. The plan found on page 20 is derived from an excavation drawing found in Guy Beresford, "Three Medieval Settlements on Dartmoor," *Medieval Archaeology* 23 (1979), pp. 98–158.

I also would like to thank the many reviewers who helped shape this book in many ways. My thanks go to the following people for their assistance: Edward Anson, University of Arkansas at Little Rock; Clifford Backman, Boston University; Daniel F. Callahan, University of Delaware; Jessica Coope, University of Nebraska; Charlotte Goldy, Miami University; Joseph Kicklighter, Auburn University; William Mathews, Potsdam College-SUNY; and Melinda Zook, Purdue University.

In writing this book, I have been inspired by my niece Nicole Bennett, who was a college student when I first thought of writing this book for college students. As a small way of expressing my gratitude for her cultural guidance and love, I dedicate this book to her.

Time present and time past
Are both perhaps present in time future
And time future contained in time past.
—T.S. Eliot
"Burnt Norton," *Four Quartets*

Contents

CHAPTER 1

Introduction

Crusaders marching off to reclaim the Holy Land; kings besieging castles with archers and men-at-arms; bishops celebrating masses in new cathedrals; merchants haggling for bargains at fairs and markets. These are the images that usually accompany any mention of the "Middle Ages." These men and their actions were important parts of medieval life, but they were also atypical. Most medieval people were not knights, kings, churchmen, or merchants. Most (more than nine out of ten) were peasants who eked out hard livings from the land. This book tells the story of one such peasant: Cecilia Penifader who lived on the English **manor** of Brigstock before the Black Death of the mid-fourteenth century.

Cecilia Penifader was born at the end of the thirteenth century; 1297 seems the most likely year. At that time, peasants were just beginning to pass surnames from one generation to the next. Cecilia's derives from *Pennyfather*, and it suggests that Cecilia's paternal grandfather or great-grandfather might have been known for his miserly habits. Perhaps the penny-pinching of her ancestors explains, in part, the prosperity of her family. Compared to knights and ladies, Cecilia's parents were poor peasants, but compared to other peasants, her parents numbered among the well-off. As a result, Cecilia grew up in a better-built cottage and with a better diet than many of her poorer neighbors. She also grew up with more siblings than most: three brothers and four sisters. When she was about twenty years old, Cecilia acquired her first bit of land in Brigstock, and for the next twenty-seven years, the records of Brigstock tell a great deal about how she acquired and used her various meadows and fields. They also reveal that she was known to her family and friends as Cissa (a name that the clerks sometimes used instead of the latinized Cecilia). These same rolls also report that Cecilia sometimes stole grain from her neighbors, sometimes argued with others, and sometimes owned animals that went astray. She never married, but she lived for about a decade next door to one brother, and she later shared a household for about five years with another brother. When she was about forty-five years old, Cecilia fell ill, and after more than a year of poor health, she died in 1344. Just before her death, she tried to give her landholdings to three young people (including one nephew and one niece), but after long and acrimonious arguments, her sister Christina inherited her properties. This is the bare outline of Cecilia's life, but the medieval archives of Brigstock tell much more.

Like other medieval peasants, Cecilia Penifader left no diaries, letters, or other personal writings. Occasionally a bright and lucky peasant learned to read and write, but most peasants were illiterate. Of the few who gained literacy, almost all were men. The most famous was Robert Grosseteste, born of poor parents about 1168, who escaped his background so thoroughly that he taught at Oxford University and rose to become Bishop of Lincoln. Yet Robert Grosseteste was exceptional. He was so intelligent, some sources say, that his surname began as a nickname—"large head"—for a precociously clever boy.

The three orders: a priest, a knight, and a peasant. Notice how the peasant is tucked into the margins of the scene, with the priest and knight turned toward each other in active conversation.

Still, his cleverness might have come to nothing. If his parents had needed him at home or if his manorial **bailiff** had opposed his education, he might never have left the place of his birth. So the educational success of Robert Grosseteste is the exception that proves the rule. Peasants, usually unable to read or write, have left no direct testimonies about their hopes, their fears, their delights, or their disappointments. Even Robert Grosseteste—who wrote a great deal about matters both philosophical and practical—never thought it worth his while to describe the world of his humble youth.

As a result, we know about peasants and their lives indirectly—from the writings of their social superiors. In the tripartite view of society that was popular by the High Middle Ages, peasants rested at the bottom of **three orders.** As "those who work" (*laboratores*), peasants supported people more privileged—"those who pray" (*oratores*) and "those who fight" (*pugnatores*). Each of these three orders ideally helped the other, with clergy contributing prayers and knights providing protection, but the mutuality of the system was more ideal than real. Also, the three groups were not equal. A peasant might have benefited from the prayers of a nun or from the protection offered by a knight, but a peasant was deemed to do work of lesser value and to be a less worthy person. Born into this unexalted state, a peasant's lot was to labor for the benefit of others. This was unfortunate for peasants, but fortunate for historians. Because peasants were important economic assets, both "those who pray" and "those who fight" kept careful records of peasant doings; today, we can use these records to reconstruct the life of an ordinary woman who was born more than seven hundred years ago.

MANORS AND MANORIAL RECORDS

Clues about how privileged people regarded peasants can be found in their courtly songs, sarcastic proverbs, nasty jokes, and pious sermons. Knights and ladies were fond of songs known as *pastourelles* that told, among other things, about how easy it was for knights to have sex with peasant women or, failing that, to rape them; monks and students enjoyed jokes that portrayed peasants as ludicrously dumb and foolish; and priests, **friars,** and bishops preached sermons that depicted "those who work" as objects of pity, charity, and disgust. Even *Piers Plowman,* a deeply sympathetic portrayal of rural life written a few decades after Cecilia Penifader's death, portrayed the peasant's lot as hard and pitiable. These literary texts are useful for understanding the often astoundingly negative attitudes of elites toward peasants, but they tell little about the peasants themselves. For information about the daily lives of peasants, the most abundant and most useful sources are legal and economic documents that report on the administration of manors.

Manorialism was the economic system whereby peasants supported the landowning elite. On manors, in other words, the working lives of peasants intersected with the financial needs of their social superiors. Manors consisted of land and tenants, and they were common in regions with fertile soils that rewarded intensive cultivation: southeast and central England, northern France, western Germany, and certain regions of southern Europe, such as the Rhône and Po valleys. The land of the manor belonged to a landowner, the lord (*dominus*) or lady (*domina*) of the manor.[1] Some manorial land—called the *demesne*—was reserved for direct use of the landowner; most was held by peasants who owed various rents and dues for their holdings.

Manorialism first developed in the Early Middle Ages, and manors were originally worked mostly by slaves and other dependent tenants. Some were descendants of the *coloni* who had once worked the villas of the Roman Empire; others had been forced into a dependent state by violence and war; and still others had surrendered themselves into bondage in return for protection. By the eleventh and twelfth centuries, slavery was disappearing in most of Europe, thanks to a combination of Church policies, opposition from peasants, and practical concessions on the part of the landowning elite. By Cecilia's time, most manors were worked by **free peasants** and **serfs** (in England, **villeins**). Freedom or serfdom was determined at birth; if born of parents who were serfs, a boy or girl was bound to serfdom. Serfs were not slaves; they could not be bought and sold at will, and they were protected by custom (that is, they were obliged to serve their manor only in the same ways that their parents had served). But because serfs were obliged not only to stay put but also to supply labor services, they provided landowners with an unusually exploitable work force for the cultivation of the demesne. In England in 1300, about half of all peasants were serfs and the other half were free.

As manors developed, they grew more economically complex. In the Early Middle Ages, manors generated profit directly: the crops peasants cultivated in the fields; the goods they produced in manorial workshops; and the rents they paid for the plots they tilled on their own. By 1300, lords and ladies profited from manors in additional ways. First, they took the produce off the demesne, and either consumed or sold it. The demesne, once cultivated by slaves, was by then usually cultivated by serfs and wage-laborers. Second, they collected rents from peasants who held plots of land from the manor. Tenants paid rent in cash, in kind (perhaps a chicken at Christmas and a few eggs at Easter), and, if serfs, in labor (under the direction of the manorial officers, serfs sowed, weeded, and harvested the demesne). Third, lords and ladies profited from legal rights that had accrued to manors over the course of centuries. Tenants had to attend manorial courts, where their small fines and fees produced valuable income; they were often obliged to pay for the use of

[1]Roughly 10 percent of manors were held by women at any one time, but this proportion varied a great deal according to time and region. Most manorial ladies were widows, who held manors as part of their **dower**—that is, as part of the properties designated to support a woman if, as often happened, her husband died before her. Widows could use dower lands to support themselves, but they usually could not sell or transfer them; after a widow died, the land went to her husband's heir. In addition to widows, some women held manors as inheritances from their parents or other kin. Inheritance customs varied throughout Europe; in some places, daughters inherited equally with sons, but in most places (including England), women usualy inherited only if they had no brothers. If an heiress did acquire a manor, she had more control over it than did a widow, for she could sell or transfer it.

manorial mills, ovens, winepresses, and other such facilities; and they had to pay a variety of small charges when they married, when they traveled, and even when they died.

Free peasants and serfs endured the burdens of manorialism because they had little choice. The economic privileges of "those who pray" and "those who fight" were buttressed by considerable military, political, and social powers. In this regard, manorialism was complemented by the culture and power of the military elite. Between the ninth and eleventh centuries, a cohort of warriors had emerged in Europe distinguished by their skill in fighting on horseback, their close ties to one another, their hereditary claims to knightly status, and their control of the land. Historians have since coined the term **feudalism** to describe the culture, relationships, and rules by which these warriors lived, but this word often generates more confusion than clarity.[2] Certainly, it implies more order, system, and standardization than was the case; the traditions of these warriors varied from place to place and were always changing to suit new circumstances. (Indeed, the adaptability of the feudal elite was an asset almost as important as their military strength.) In the England into which Cecilia was born at the end of the thirteenth century, a small feudal elite, headed by a king, ruled the land. They waged war and negotiated peace; they judged and punished wrongdoers; they decided who could pass through their territories. In short, they governed by virtue of their wealth, aristocratic birth, and military might. Peasants were taught to respect the authority of the feudal elite as natural and good, but respectful demeanor was a practical matter too. Faced with a powerful and arrogant knight, Cecilia—or any other peasant— usually found that deference and obedience were the safest behaviors.

To profit from manors, lords and ladies needed not only to wield power effectively but also to manage their manors efficiently. In the late eighth century, Charlemagne, king of the Franks, had sought to compile detailed lists of royal manors, and in the ninth century, registers of lands, tenants, and income were kept for some ecclesiastical estates. But it was in England in the thirteenth century that the most developed systems of manorial record-keeping developed. There, an array of stewards, bailiffs, **reeves,** clerks, and other manorial officers supervised manors, and they kept copious records to prove that they were conscientious and honest administrators (and, in some cases, to hide their cheating). These records tell a great deal about the peasants with

---

[2]*Feudalism* is a word with two distinctive—and potentially confusing—meanings. Some scholars use it to describe the general economy of the Middle Ages; to them, feudalism is a stage in economic development in which serfs on manors were forced to labor on behalf of a warrior class. This stage is seen as falling between slavery and capitalism. Many students encounter this definition of feudalism—which derives from the writings of Karl Marx—in economics and sociology courses. But most historians use feudalism in the more limited sense employed in this book; that is, to describe the customs and relationships of an elite who governed ordinary people by virtue of their military, political, and social power. Feudalism is a modern word; a medieval person would probably have talked about *vassalage*. For arguments against the concept of feudalism, see E. A. R. Brown, "The Tyranny of a Concept: Feudalism and Historians of Medieval Europe," *American Historical Review* 79 (1974), 1063–88, and Susan Reynolds, *Fiefs and Vassals: The Medieval Evidence Reinterpreted* (1994).

whom manorial officers dealt on a regular basis. *Custumals* detailed the customs of a manor. In Brigstock, for example, a custumal specified that a sick person who gave away land had to be strong enough to leave his or her house after the gift; if the grantor died without so doing, the transfer was invalid. This rule ensured that no dying persons could be pressured to preempt, on their death-beds, the claims of heirs. *Surveys* and *rentals* listed the tenants of the manor, telling what lands they held and, in the case of rentals, what rents (in cash, kind, or labor) they owed. No such records survive for Brigstock in Cecilia's day, but a rental from 1416—about seventy years after her death—suggests that her family fortunes had plummeted; not a single Penifader was listed among the tenants of the manor. *Account rolls* noted the expenses and profits of a manor, usually for a year starting at Michaelmas (29 September), the traditional end of the harvest season. No complete accounts survive for medieval Brigstock, but, if they did, they might tell about the stipends given to manorial servants or the wages paid to workers hired on a day-basis to do specific tasks. *Court rolls* describe the proceedings of manorial courts, which dealt with a wide variety of contracts, disputes, and petty crimes. These usually met either twice a year or, as in Brigstock, every three weeks.[3] When court rolls survive in abundance—as they do for Brigstock in the late thirteenth and early fourteenth centuries—they offer unparalleled information about the crime, controversy, and commerce among medieval peasants.

During Cecilia Penifader's lifetime, almost all members of the feudal and ecclesiastical elite in England relied on manors and peasants for some of their support. When kings, queens, barons, ladies, bishops, monks, and nuns sat down to supper, they ate food produced by the labor of serfs on manorial demesnes. When they purchased fine silks from the East, built new houses in stone, or arranged to have wine shipped from Gascony, they spent money accumulated from the rents, fees, and fines of their manorial tenants, free and serf. Yet the manor was not the only point of fiscal intersection between peasants and their social superiors. Monarchs held manors of their own, but they also claimed some authority over *all* peasants within their realms—even those who lived on manors owned by others. In England, the king could tax all peasants, could compel male peasants to join his armies, and could even force peasants to sell him animals or food at set prices. Cecilia Penifader was unfortunate to live in a time of particularly harsh royal exactions, a time when the

---

[3]Historians use the term "roll" to describe manorial records because that is exactly what they are; after clerks finished writing their notes on parchment, they rolled them up. Since clerks usually also stitched together many parchment sheets (or *membranes*) to form a single roll, account rolls and court rolls can be very fat. In Brigstock in 1314–15, for example, 13 sheets of parchment (most between 12 and 24 inches long) were joined end-to-end to produce a single roll of more than 19 feet. On this roll, the clerk kept notes for 16 courts held between November 1314 and September 1315. Sometimes it is awkward to read these rolls, but medieval clerks knew what they were doing. Rolled into compact bundles, these rolls could be easily transported and stored. The parchment used in making manorial rolls came from the skins of animals, usually sheep. Parchment was expensive to use, but durable. In the century or so after Cecilia's death, paper became more common in Europe, and in many cases, later records kept on paper have rotted more quickly than earlier ones kept on parchment.

Photograph by Peter Moyse, A.R.P.S.

The Brigstock court roll for 1314–15. This roll is made up of 13 sheets of parchment stitched together end-to-end, and it measures more than 19 feet in length.

three Edwards—Edward I (1272–1307), his son Edward II (1307–1327), and his grandson Edward III (1327–1377)—turned repeatedly to ordinary peasants to find money, men, and food for their wars in Wales, Scotland, and France.

Bishops, monks, and nuns were also supported by manors, and like monarchs, they had further interests in the peasants who lived outside their episcopal palaces and monastic walls. In common with all medieval Christians, peasants were compelled to **tithe,** which meant that each year one-tenth of their harvested grain, new lambs, and other produce was given to the Church. Peasants were also subject to ecclesiastical jurisdiction, and, if brought into a church court for fornication, slander, bigamy, or other offenses that fell under Church supervision, they could face fines and physical punishments. Some peasants so angered Church officers that they even endured excommunication, that is, they were cut off from participation in the sacraments and community of the Church. In January 1299, for example, the Bishop of Lincoln ordered the excommunication of everyone in Brigstock who had participated in a robbery the week before. The thieves had secretly entered the chamber of Hugh Wade, a lodger in the house of a local widow, and stolen money and goods out of his strongbox. More than likely, the Bishop responded so strongly to this theft because Hugh Wade may have been a cleric or servant of the Bishop (or both). It was in the interest of monarchs and ecclesiastics to keep good records of these additional dealings with peasants. Wherever tax lists, military requisitions, ecclesiastical court books, or bishops' registers survive, they provide further information about the lives of ordinary people in the medieval countryside. As with manorial documentation, so too with these other types of records: they are especially full and abundant for England in the thirteenth and fourteenth centuries.[4]

In short, we can study medieval peasants because their labor was so important in supporting the Church, the monarchy, and the landed elite. Although all records pertaining to manors and peasants are useful, the most useful are manorial court rolls. Peasants brought most of their legal business to these courts. Although free peasants could take some complaints to county or royal courts and serious crimes (such as murder and rape) often had to be judged in higher courts, it was to manorial courts that most rural disputes, crimes, inheritances, and contracts were reported. The court records for the manor of Brigstock survive in exceptional number for the time of Cecilia Penifader: 549 courts held between 1287 and 1348. It is important to recognize, at the outset, that manorial courts were different from modern courts. Today, most of us go to court only when forced by special crisis or summons; in the fourteenth century, Cecilia Penifader and other tenants in Brigstock attended court every three weeks, accepting its meetings as an ordinary and expected obligation. Today, we usually go to court for unpleasant reasons, especially to resolve conflicts or crimes; Cecilia and her neighbors certainly raised such difficulties in their court, but they also registered agreements, exchanged land, and agreed on ordinances. Today, courts are dominated by professional lawyers without whom almost nothing can be done; the peasants of Brigstock were so fully conversant with the rules of their courts that they seldom needed specialists to help them. The meeting of a manorial court was so ordinary a part of life in Brigstock that most people probably felt as comfortable in court as they did in church or in the lanes in front of their houses. Special court buildings were rarely constructed, so when peasants attended court, they literally gathered at their local church, in the lane, on the green, or at some other familiar location.

In its origins, a manorial court was an instrument of seignorial power, a way for the lord or lady to control the manor's tenants and to extract income

[4]In some cases, the superiority of English records seems to stem from the more careful record-keeping of administrators in medieval England, but, in most cases, it has been mostly a matter of survival through the centuries. Thanks to a strong legal system and a relatively stable social order, England's medieval archives have survived especially well. In France, for contrast, many medieval archives were destroyed during the French Revolution.

from them. In actual practice, especially by Cecilia's day, peasants used manorial courts for their own purposes, and the courts reflected local customs as well as the landowner's interests. In a sense, the manor was the institution that convened the courts and kept records of the proceedings, but another institution, the peasant community, helped to determine what actually happened at any meeting. If jurors did not want to tell the court that a young woman had broken into the manorial sheepfold, then she could get away unpunished. If local custom determined that youngest sons inherited their fathers' lands instead of oldest sons, then no lord or lady could go against that tradition in court. If tenants were unhappy about an action taken by a manorial officer, they would not hesitate to complain in court and even seek redress. So when Cecilia Penifader and her neighbors gathered every three weeks for the meeting of the Brigstock court, they were unlikely to be awed or alienated by the proceedings. Some peasants were more active and powerful in the court than others, but most probably saw it as a necessary burden and a useful forum; through it, they resolved conflicts, punished assaults and crimes, registered inheritances and transfers of land, checked that brewers and bakers did not cheat their customers, recorded loans and other contracts, and otherwise managed the day-to-day life of their community.

BRIGSTOCK AND CECILIA PENIFADER

In the early fourteenth century, there were thousands of rural communities scattered across the landscape of Europe. Neighboring **villages** could be quite different from each other, and differences between the regions of Europe were even more striking. As a result, Brigstock, the community in which Cecilia Penifader lived for almost fifty years, certainly does not represent The Medieval Manor. In Italy, for example, settlement was more continuous with Roman traditions than was the case in England; manorialism relied less on labor services and more on cash rents; and drier soils required different tools, different crop rotations, and different crops. In the Holy Roman Empire, for another example, as German lords sought to colonize lands east of the Elbe in the eleventh and twelfth centuries, they offered special privileges to attract settlers; as a result, peasants in these newly colonized areas enjoyed extensive freedoms and low rents that would have been the envy of their counterparts elsewhere. Brigstock does not even represent *English* communities, for to the north of Brigstock lay areas where hamlets were more common than villages and manorial authority was lightly felt; to the east lay East Anglia, renowned for its intensive and sophisticated techniques of farming; and in Devon and Cornwall to the southwest, there were few communities that closely resembled Brigstock in either manorial structure or economy. In much the same way, Cecilia cannot represent The Medieval Peasant. Many peasants were poorer than she; many were male, rather than female; and most married, but she never did.

The location of Brigstock in Europe.

No village or person could possibly represent 90 percent of the medieval population, and Brigstock and Cecilia were, at least, not wildly atypical. Brigstock, located in the heart of the most manorialized part of England, provides an especially fine example of the intersection of manor, village, and **parish**, and Cecilia's life, supplemented by the lives of her married brothers and sisters, offers an unusually clear view of the opportunities and choices that women and men faced in rural communities. Moreover, Brigstock and Cecilia are exceptionally well-documented, a fact of no small importance when studying humble people who lived many centuries ago. Still, Cecilia's life is best read as a case study, not a universal example. In some ways, she was quite common, average, and perhaps even representative; in other ways, her story was uniquely her own. Sometimes typical and sometimes not, Cecilia's life is fascinating on its own terms. It allows us to approach, in an intimate way, the ordinary life of one ordinary medieval person.

Brigstock is located in the English midlands, about seventy-five miles north of London. Today, Brigstock lies in open country, but in the Middle Ages, it rested in the heart of Rockingham Forest, a royal preserve for hunting. For Cecilia, this meant that near her house stood not only fields and pastures but also a royal hunting lodge, woodlands, and parks maintained by the king's foresters. These officers allowed the people of Brigstock to use the woods and parks in some agreed-upon ways, such as collecting fallen wood for fuel and feeding their pigs in the woods. Yet the king's foresters also stood ready to arrest any peasant who tried to hunt game in Rockingham Forest or attempted to clear bits of the forest to bring new lands under the plow. In 1255, for example, the foresters searched for Hugh Swartgar and Henry Tuke of Brigstock, suspected of placing nets in the forest for catching hares; both men were eventually caught, judged guilty, and imprisoned. Like most forest communities, Brigstock's economy was diverse and flexible. Cecilia's neighbors supported themselves primarily by farming and animal husbandry, but they also profited from poaching, charcoal-making, and fishing. Some also worked in trades such as carpentry, thatching, and brewing, and a few seem to have taken on industrial work, such as making pots, weaving thread into cloth, and quarrying stone.

In Cecilia's day, Brigstock consisted of three overlapping institutions: village, manor, and parish. The **village** of Brigstock was the oldest of the three, for long before there were manors or parishes, the peasants of Europe had settled themselves on the land. There is some evidence of Roman activity in Brigstock, but it was probably during the period of Anglo-Saxon settlement in the fifth and sixth centuries that people first came to the area, settled in a cluster of houses, and began to clear the surrounding fields. When these first settlers built their houses huddled together in a central location in Brigstock, they formed one common sort of rural community in the Middle Ages—a *nucleated village*. Elsewhere, peasants established different types of settlements. Some lived on farmsteads scattered through the countryside, each settled on its own plot of land, and some lived in small hamlets, with a few households in a single location. These alternative forms of settlement were common in England and Europe, especially in regions of difficult terrain or poor soil. Brigstock's nucleated village was typical of settlement in the English midlands, and it was found in other parts of northern Europe where soils were rich enough to support many families at once.

The **manor** of Brigstock was much bigger than the village itself. In 1086, the clerks of William I completed the **Domesday Book,** a survey of the manors, landowners, and tenants in his newly conquered realm of England. Brigstock manor then comprised almost all of the village of Brigstock and parts of three other settlements—much of Stanion to the northwest, and small parts of Geddington to the southwest and Islip to the southeast. Stanion was particularly important, for it had been created, sometime before 1086, when men and women from Brigstock decided to carve out new lands deeper in the forest. In Cecilia Penifader's time, Stanion and Brigstock remained closely tied. Her parents held lands in both villages, as did almost all of their children once they grew up.

Brigstock was also part of a **parish,** but like Brigstock manor, the parish was bigger than Brigstock village. A church dedicated to St. Andrew stood at the center of Brigstock, and it was an important focal point for the community. People worshipped in the church of St. Andrew not only on Sunday but also on holy days. Their faith was mixed with pre-Christian customs and practices, and it was profound and heartfelt; there were no atheists in medieval Brigstock, nor in any other medieval villages or towns. Moreover, as the biggest and sturdiest building in Brigstock, the church of St. Andrew was a place of work and play, as well as a place of worship. People held meetings in its nave, stored grain in its driest corners, and sold goods in its churchyard. The priest assigned to the church of St. Andrew had numerous and important duties, but he also had a second set of responsibilities: the church of St. Peter in Stanion was designated as a dependent chapel within the parish of Brigstock. In other words, the parish of Brigstock embraced two villages, Brigstock and Stanion, and two churches, St. Andrew's and St. Peter's. For most purposes, the people of Stanion worshipped in their own church, but on major feast days such as Christmas, Easter, and the feast of St. Andrew, they probably walked the few miles to Brigstock to celebrate in St. Andrew's, the main church of the parish.

For Cecilia Penifader, these institutions—village, manor, and parish—were very real. She agreed with other villagers on when to plant and when to harvest; she paid fines and fees at the manorial court; she rendered her tithe to the parish. It might often have seemed to her as if village, manor, and parish blended one into another. Parish funds could be used to repair a village bridge; manorial courts met on rainy days in the nave of St. Andrew's church; villagers worked together to meet manorial obligations. But the three entities did not neatly coincide, and, with its messily overlapping boundaries of manor, parish, and village, Brigstock was typical of many rural communities, in England and elsewhere. As economic and ecclesiastical districts laid upon the already settled patterns of villages, the boundaries of manors and parishes were drawn according to their own logic. In a world where villages had been settled by peasants, manors created to support the landed elite, and parishes drawn to care for Christian souls, boundaries of village, manor, and parish were sometimes coterminous, but often not.

THE PLAN OF THE BOOK

The chapters that follow begin with Cecilia's childhood and end with her death, but they are organized topically rather than chronologically. We begin with three chapters that examine the main institutions of Cecilia's life: the homes, lanes, and fields of her native place; the manor under whose authority she was born and lived; and the parish that nurtured her faith through the years. In laying a critical foundation, these chapters allow us to imagine Cecilia in the context of village, manor, and parish. In chapter 5, we will turn to what was probably the most traumatic experience of Cecilia's life, a famine that afflicted Brigstock and most of northern Europe between 1315 and 1322. In the years when Cecilia was coming of age, she saw many of her neighbors and probably also her father and mother suffer from hunger, sicken, and die. But Cecilia herself survived the Great Famine and, as we shall see, even profited from the greater distress of her neighbors. In subsequent chapters, we will explore further aspects of her story: how her relations with parents, siblings, and kin evolved over the course of her life; how she supported herself through labor, land, and trade; how she stood in relation to her neighbors and fellow tenants; and finally, how her female gender did and did not shape her experiences. We will end by assessing what Cecilia Penifader's life can tell us about the medieval world in which she lived and the modern world from which we observe her history.

SUGGESTIONS FOR FURTHER READING

The best introductions to medieval rural society are: Werner Rösener, *Peasants in the Middle Ages* (1992), much stronger on German states than elsewhere; Robert Fossier, *Peasant Life in the Medieval West* (1988) and Georges Duby, *Rural Economy and Country Life in the Medieval West* (1968), both strongest on France; and Edward Miller and John Hatcher, *Medieval England: Rural Society and Economic Change 1086–1348* (1978). These books provide information about the many issues developed in later chapters of this book. Emmanuel Le Roy Ladurie's study of heretics in an early fourteenth-century village, *Montaillou: The Promised Land of Error* (1978), offers a lively look at one village in the southernmost part of France. H. S. Bennett's *Life on the English Manor: A Study of Peasant Conditions, 1150–1400* (1937) and George C. Homans' *English Villagers of the Thirteenth Century* (1941) are outdated, but readable.

P. D. A. Harvey's *Manorial Records* (1984) provides an excellent introduction to the documents that are so important in studying the English peasantry. J. Ambrose Raftis' pathbreaking study *Tenure and Mobility: Studies in the Social History of the Mediaeval English Village* (1964) provides abstracts from court rolls and analyses of their content.

CHAPTER 2

The World Around Her

Cecilia Penifader was first mentioned in the Brigstock court in August 1316, when she was still living at home under the authority of her father Robert Penifader. Richard Everard complained that Cecilia and her father had gone into his part of the Northmeadow, ignored his boundary stones, and taken hay from his land. Robert Penifader responded that these charges were false, and he promised to prove his claim. No final resolution of this dispute was ever written into the court record.

Cecilia Penifader was born into a sizable and prosperous family in Brigstock village, or more likely, the adjacent village of Stanion (then part of Brigstock manor).[1] Her parents, Robert and Alice, had a large number of children, at least three sons and five daughters. Two children, Emma and Alice, seem to have died young, and only one child, Christina, lived long enough to witness the horrors of the Black Death when it arrived in Brigstock in 1349. Although it is impossible to reconstruct precise patterns of birth and infant mortality from medieval records, it is clear that the Penifaders were fecund and fortunate. If Cecilia's mother married her father at the usual age of about 20, she would have had 20 fertile years to produce her family (medieval women rarely bore children in their forties). Bearing eight children in two decades, she

---

[1] Robert and Alice Penifader held land in the villages of Brigstock and Stanion, as did Cecilia once she grew up. As a grown woman, Cecilia lived in Stanion, and it is likely that her parents had done the same when she was a child. Brigstock and Stanion were tied together in so many ways that I shall do as Cecilia and her neighbors themselves did, that is, treat the two settlements as the single community of Brigstock. Whenever necessary, distinctions will be drawn between the manor, parish, and village of Brigstock.

THE PENIFADERS OF BRIGSTOCK

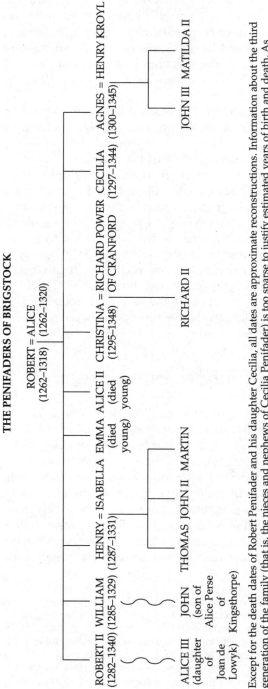

ROBERT = ALICE
(1262–1318) | (1262–1320)

ROBERT II WILLIAM
(1282–1340) (1285–1329)

HENRY = ISABELLA
(1287–1331)

EMMA ALICE II
(died   (died
young) young)

CHRISTINA = RICHARD POWER
(1295–1348) OF CRANFORD

CECILIA
(1297–1344)

AGNES = HENRY KROYL
(1300–1345)

ALICE III
(daughter
of
Joan de
Lowyk)

JOHN
(son of
Alice Perse
of
Kingsthorpe)

THOMAS JOHN II MARTIN

RICHARD II

JOHN III MATILDA II

Except for the death dates of Robert Penifader and his daughter Cecilia, all dates are approximate reconstructions. Information about the third generation of the family (that is, the nieces and nephews of Cecilia Penifader) is too sparse to justify estimated years of birth and death. As indicated by wavy lines, the children of Robert II and William were illegitimate.

followed a biologically predictable pattern; if a peasant wife used no effective birth control and nursed her infants (an activity that delayed the resumption of menstruation), she usually gave birth at intervals of about 2½ years. Aristocratic women, who not only married at younger ages but also employed wet-nurses, usually produced larger numbers of children. Eleanor of Castile, who married Edward I when she was about 10 years old, bore 15 (or possibly 16) children; Philippa of Hainault, who married Edward III at the age of 14 years, gave birth to twelve children.[2]

Bearing eight children in 20 years, Alice Penifader made the most of her fertility as a nursing mother, and she seems never to have tried to prevent or terminate a pregnancy. This was not through lack of knowledge. Medieval women knew about a wide variety of plants that could discourage conception or sometimes induce early abortion. Their concoctions were not as effective as methods used today, but they sometimes worked. Artemisia, which inhibits ovulation, and rue, which causes uterine contractions, were among the plants readily available to women in Brigstock. Alice seems never to have resorted to such measures, but many women did. In addition to producing many children, Alice and her husband Robert were also lucky enough to beat the odds of infant and child mortality. In most medieval villages, almost half of all children died before reaching adulthood, but most of the children of Alice and Robert grew to full age. All in all, the Penifader household was atypical. Most of their neighbors in Brigstock, like most peasant couples, produced only three children who survived them.

HOUSE AND FARMYARD

Cecilia was the seventh of eight children, born into a house filled with three brothers and three sisters. This house was probably comfortable by Brigstock standards but humble by the standards of our day. Like all the houses in Brigstock, it was dark. Some houses had no windows, but the Penifaders, as well-off tenants, might have cut a window or two into their walls. If so, the windows had no glass, and only shutters kept out the wind and cold. Like all the houses in Brigstock, the Penifader house was filled with smoke. A fire was essential for warmth and cooking, but, as chimneys were unknown among peasants, smoke was vented through a hole in the roof. Perhaps the Penifaders, like others who could afford it, built an especially high roof to draw up the

---

[2]The use of wet-nurses, women paid to breast-feed the infants of others, was common in Europe and many other parts of the world until recently; if an infant's mother could not or would not provide milk, then a wet-nurse was the only alternative. In the early twentieth century, when the vulcanization of rubber made artificial nipples and bottle-feeding more feasible, wet-nursing declined in importance in Europe. Many wet-nurses had milk because their own infants had died, but others nursed two children at once. Sometimes wet-nurses lived in the households of their employers (especially when the employers were aristocrats); sometimes infants were sent away to spend their early years in the homes of wet-nurses. For more information on this subject, see Valerie A. Fildes, *Wet Nursing: A History from Antiquity to the Present* (1988).

The interior of a peasant house.

smoke to the hole in its apex; this strategy eased the smokiness. Finally, like all the houses in Brigstock, the house in which Cecilia grew up was small. Peasant houses were usually twice as long as their width, and a prosperous family like the Penifaders probably lived in a house about 30 feet by 15 feet. Dark, smoky, and cramped, peasant houses were not welcoming places. It was no wonder people usually preferred, weather permitting, to sit outside on benches set against the walls of their homes.

Until recently, a stone house that perhaps dated back to Cecilia's day stood in Brigstock. Its walls were built of rubble, not stone blocks, but even this was fine by the standards of the early fourteenth century. Most medieval peasants used rubble only for a low foundation a foot or two off the ground; they then built the walls by placing posts every few feet and filling in the gaps with wattle and daub, that is, sticks and twigs woven together with the gaps

A man drying his feet and shoes over a fire which is also being used both for cooking (notice the pot) and for smoking meat and sausages (hung from a bar above).

filled by clay, straw, moss, and other such materials. (Sometimes these walls were so flimsy that robbers literally broke into a house by avoiding the locked door and forcing entry through the walls.) Set at a low point in the walls of the Brigstock house were crucks, long curved timbers, that rose up to brace the wall and hold the roof. The roof was straw thatch; this was cheap and easy for medieval peasants and prone to disastrous fire. A house like this would have been built, as Cecilia's likely was, with a combination of family labor and hired labor. If a family could afford it, they were especially likely to hire skilled workers to lay the foundation, erect the timber frame, and set the thatch.

The interior of the medieval house that until recently stood in Brigstock had a second floor, but this was a later addition. In Cecilia's house, there would have been one floor only, a packed dirt floor, possibly covered with straw. Perhaps boards laid across braces of the crucks provided, at one end of the house, a loft for storage or extra sleeping. Furnishings were minimal: benches or stools for sitting; a trestle table that could be put away when not in use; a chest to hold bedding, towels, and other linens; a cupboard to hold jugs, bowls, and spoons. All these would have been pushed against the walls. When it was time to eat, the table would be unfolded, the bowls and spoons set out, the benches put in place. The Penifaders' diet was simple. Parents and children ate bread and drank weak ale at every meal, and they also ate, whenever available, such other foods as bacon, sausages, cheeses, eggs, fish, onions, leeks, garlic, cabbages, apples, and pears. When it was time to sleep, the tables and benches were set aside, and bedding (at best, a cloth bag stuffed with either straw or chaff from threshed oats) was laid out in their place. The one immovable feature of the interior was the hearth, set in the center of the house, with its pots and trivets; it was around the hearth that everyone sat, ate, and slept. Perhaps the Penifaders' house, like the main floor of the now demolished Brigstock house, was partitioned to create a small room on one side. This room was probably used for storage and sleeping; it offered a bit of privacy, but it was far from the hearth in winter.

Cecilia, in other words, grew up in a house that provided the essentials of life: a hearth for cooking and warmth; a shelter from wind, rain, and snow; a place to eat and sleep. But her house was not a place to linger, and whenever she could, Cecilia probably wandered into the farmyard around her house where her parents and siblings also spent much of their time. Sometimes houses stood together along a street, built with shared walls, and in such cases, farmyards ran behind the houses. More often, however, houses stood separately within their farmyards; in these cases, most of the farmyard ran behind the house, but some of it could also lie in front and along the sides. The farmyard was a large area, perhaps an acre or more, closed off by fences or ditches from street, lane, and neighbors.[3] In the Penifader farmyard, Cecilia sat with her family in the early evening, assisted her mother in many tasks, or watched over the safekeeping of some of the household animals. (In the winter, cows, pigs, chickens, and other animals were often taken into the house to protect them from the elements and to add to the warmth of the interior. But animals were usually kept in the farmyard, sometimes in a barn.) The farmyard was a social place, especially in front of the house, where Cecilia probably found benches for sitting, fences for leaning, and a cobbled space for games. She amused herself in ways that echo the play of modern children—by imitating the work of her parents, by dancing and singing, by chasing animals or wandering about the farmyard, by playing ball or other organized games, and by creating imaginary worlds with other children. The farmyard was also a place for storage: perhaps a barn for animals, a shed for tools or grain, a well or cistern for rainwater, a haystack or two, and certainly, at some distance from the house if possible, a dung heap where human and animal waste was carefully accumulated for spreading as fertilizer on the fields.

Most importantly, the farmyard was a place of work, especially work for women and children. Cecilia's mother baked bread and brewed ale in the farmyard; she milked cows and made cheese; she took advantage of outdoor light to mend old clothes and stitch new ones; she tended a beehive; she collected eggs from her roosting hens; she fattened her pigs; she cared for a few apple and pear trees; she cultivated a garden that yielded onions, turnips, peas, beans, leeks, garlic, cabbages, and herbs. The farmyards of Brigstock, small, readily fertilized, easily worked on an intermittent basis, and free of any communal regulation, were the most intensely cultivated lands in the community. The products that came from farmyards were valued by everyone, for the variety they brought to the diet and for their marketability. In collecting eggs, making ale, and cultivating onions, Alice Penifader not only fed her family but also earned some cash by selling foodstuffs to her neighbors or at nearby markets.

As Cecilia grew up in the house and farmyard of her parents, she followed hygienic practices that today might seem crude. Bathing was rare, not only because of fears of drowning but also because baths were considered unhealthy—liable to lead to colds, fevers, or worse. On occasion, she splashed herself with water and soap, but more often than not, cleanliness meant clean hands, clean face, and little more. She also had no toilet, and she either walked out to the dung heap in the farmyard or used a bucket that was occasionally emptied on

---

[3]An acre measures 43,560 square feet, that is, about 75 percent of a football field in the United States.

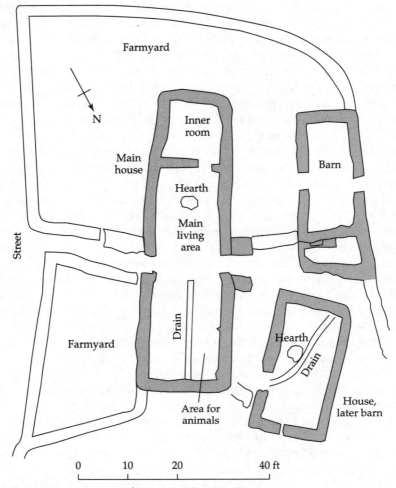

Excavation drawing of a peasant house and farmyard.

the dung heap. Like her parents and siblings, Cecilia wore simple clothes: stockings and leather shoes; long gowns (men wore shorter tunics); and for warmth in the winter, coats or cloaks (both outfitted with hoods). Made of undyed wool, all clothing fitted loosely. This made it slightly easier for Alice Penifader to clothe her family by stitching a new cloak or altering an old one for a hand-me-down.

ARABLE, PASTURE, STREAM, AND FOREST

Outside the immediate house and farmyard of her family, Cecilia found a large and diverse community. Brigstock lay in the heart of Rockingham Forest, a royal preserve for hunting. The Norman kings William II (1087–1100) and Henry I (1100–1135) hunted in the forest and maintained a lodge at Brigstock for their use. Built of wood, it consisted of a hall, a chamber, and a stable. As far as we know, no kings visited the lodge after Henry I, but they kept it in good repair; Cecilia might have stared at these buildings and crept around them as a child. By the late fourteenth century, however, the lodge had fallen into ruin, and it was so thoroughly demolished that modern archaeologists have not yet succeeded in pinpointing its location. Local tradition holds that the manor house that now stands in Brigstock, an imposing structure of fine stone blocks built about 1500, rests on the site of the timber lodge of Cecilia's day.

Brigstock and Stanion today are thriving villages, clustered in a gently rolling landscape. Both settlements are nucleated, that is, with all the houses gathered into a central location. In Cecilia's time, the Penifaders and their neighbors had already settled along the same main streets of Brigstock and Stanion that can be seen today, but their lives were different and much less prosperous from the lives of those who now inhabit these villages. The peasants of fourteenth-century Brigstock relied on an *economy of makeshifts,* an economy that required them to respond flexibly to any opportunity that arose.[4] They had, in other words, to juggle many tasks and to make do with whatever materials, cash, and work they could find. Peasants often relied a bit on wages earned by working for others or on profits gained from selling ale, bread, wool, or other commodities, but they especially relied on what they could produce from the land. Two anchors kept this highly flexible economy going—first, the arable fields on which peasants grew wheat, barley, rye, oats, and other crops; and second, the meadows and pastures that fed their sheep, horses, and oxen.

Like many medieval communities, Brigstock had **open fields** that were plowed, sown, weeded, harvested, and left **fallow** (that is, unplanted) according to common agreement. Brigstock had several such fields (each given a local name), and the Penifaders held bits of land in most of them. The arable lands of Cecilia's parents were spread through several fields around the manor—a half-acre here, a parcel there, another half-acre over there. (When Cecilia grew up she too would hold land scattered about the manor. In 1335, for example, she acquired an acre of arable that was distributed in three locations. As described in the court roll, they were found under the "Sale," in "Stitches," and "between the Valkmill and the new dyke.") Every year, the Penifaders' use of each small bit of land, whether they planted it with wheat or rye in the autumn, or oats, barley, or beans in the spring, or left it fallow, was determined by the common agreement of all tenants. Robert and Alice, in other words, were not able to sit on their front bench and plan what to plant where and when; instead, they had to use their land in ways agreed on by their neighbors. This system of agriculture is different from the large blocks of land, farmed by single owners, that now dot the landscape of Europe. Yet it made good sense at the time.

---

[4]A "makeshift" is an expedient, a temporary way of managing. It comes from the expression "to make shift," meaning to get along as best one can. Olwen Hufton coined the term "economy of makeshifts" to describe the survival strategies of the poor during the ancien régime. See her much acclaimed book, *The Poor of Eighteenth-Century France, 1750–1789* (1974).

First, consider that many households held lands scattered throughout the fields of a manor, rather than compactly consolidated into one family farm. This arrangement is sometimes called **strip** farming because each field was divided into strips tended by different families. Scattering a family's lands had several advantages. It spread risk, for if crops in one field had a bad year, crops in another might do fine; it facilitated the sharing of plows and draft animals, for several households could pool their resources to plow a field containing their strips; and it encouraged parental generosity to children, for instead of a block of family land that had to be held together for a single heir, parents held many strips that could, if they wished and their bailiff allowed, be more easily dispersed among many children.

Second, consider that boundaries between strips were unfenced (hence the term *open field*). Although peasants did not use fences in the open fields, they nevertheless marked boundaries between strips, usually with stones or other low markers of the sort that Richard Everard accused Cecilia and her father of ignoring in the court case that opens this chapter. Boundary stones could be moved as well as ignored, and this was a serious offense. If one household could thereby gain a foot or two of land, it gained a great deal, especially if stones were moved ever so slightly again and again. Despite such problems, boundary stones were preferred for one reason: fencing would have obstructed the movement of plows during planting and animals eating stubble after harvest. With boundary stones lying close to the ground, more of the land could be cultivated more easily.

Third, consider that tenants had to cooperate with each other over how a field containing the strips of many people might be used. This limited individual initiative, but it was essential. If the Penifaders had decided to plant oats in a field where everyone else had planted wheat the autumn before, they would have created havoc. In the early spring, when they would have needed to prepare their strip for sowing oats, they would have dragged their plow through the maturing wheat of their neighbors. This would have made the Penifaders few friends and many enemies. Cooperation was eased by custom. It was not as if everyone had to debate every year about the use of every field; there was a set pattern of rotation that everyone expected and therefore more easily observed. By Cecilia's time, many open-field villages in England had adopted a three-field course of rotation. Peasants planted one field with a winter crop (wheat or rye) sown in the autumn, cultivated a spring crop (oats, barley, peas, or beans) on the second, and let the third field lie fallow. Every year they rotated the use of the fields; the winter field would then have a spring crop, the spring field lay fallow, and the fallow field was sown with wheat. The **three-field system** was an innovation of the High Middle Ages, and it improved on a variety of less efficient rotations, especially the **two-field system** (in which half the land was fallow at any one time). In the eleventh century, many villages in Northern Europe began to shift from a two-field rotation to one based on three fields. But the change was a slow one; in Cecilia's day, the three-field system was used in Brigstock but probably not in Stanion. Although Stanion did eventually adopt a three-field rotation, many other places did not. In villages with poor soils and in Mediterranean villages, where summers were too hot for spring crops, the three-field rotation was not feasible. On the rich plains of the north (including the midlands of England), however, the three-field system helped peasants not only to minimize fallow but also to sow a valuable second crop in the spring.

Fourth, consider that peasants left large portions of arable land—usually one-third or one-half—untilled every year. Fallowing was common because animal and human waste was insufficient for fertilizing the land, and few other alternatives were available. Since fallow land naturally replenished itself, the Penifaders and their neighbors carefully left each field untilled every two or three years. Also, they made sure that sheep grazed the stubble from the harvest and that other animals were turned out onto the fallow. The droppings from these animals helped further to replenish the soil. In many communities, fallow fields and pastures were considered to be **common lands** available for the flocks and herds of everyone, and in such instances, villagers often carefully specified how many animals each household could place on these commons. This was so that no single tenant could, as the Brigstock custumal of 1391 stated, "overcharge the commons."

The arable land of Brigstock was important and closely regulated, but it accounted for only one-fourth of the land of the manor. Most of the rest was given to the second anchor of Brigstock's economy: *pastures* in which animals grazed and grassy *meadows* used either as hayfields or for further grazing. These lands were also held in parcels scattered through many fields. Elsewhere in England and Europe, some peasants supported themselves almost exclusively with animal husbandry, particularly if they lived in mountainous regions or areas with poor soils. In Brigstock, where the landscape rolled only gently and the soil richly repaid cultivation, animals still contributed critically to the economy. Horses and oxen pulled wagons and carried burdens; sheep produced wool that could be marketed to local merchants; cows and goats gave milk that could be turned into cheese (people rarely drank milk); pigs were raised especially for their meat. These animals supported peasant families directly with their wool, milk, and meat, and indirectly through their contributions to arable husbandry; their waste fertilized the fields, and their pulling power enabled peasants to plow those fields. As a result, the rural economy of villages such as Brigstock and Stanion is best considered an economy of *mixed farming*. Peasants raised crops and animals, and the two activities supported each other. No animals meant infertile fields; infertile fields meant no stubble for animals to feed on.

When Cecilia walked around Brigstock and saw open fields given over to arable, pasture, and meadow, she saw something else as well, especially on the outskirts of the fields. She saw small parcels of land, enclosed by fences or ditches, each of which belonged entirely to one family. The Penifaders might have held several of these, and if so, they called them, as did everyone else in Brigstock, *newsets* or, more commonly, *assarts*. The first word gives an important clue about how these private enclosures were formed, for they were newly cultivated lands, created when a family or a group of families decided to fell trees, clear land, and put it to productive use. Sometimes this was done surreptitiously; Brigstock peasants sometimes cleared edges of Rockingham Forest, doubtless hoping, often correctly, that the king's foresters would either not notice or not care. Sometimes it was done with license, for holders of unproductive land were often delighted to see it cleared and, of course, to collect new rents on it. In either case, the assart was usually enclosed, kept distinct from the open fields, and used—like the farmyard around the house—for whatever purposes a family might choose.[5]

Running through the fields and assarts of Brigstock was another important resource for Cecilia and her family. Harper's Brook, which created the small valley in which Brigstock lay, yielded fish available to everyone. It was also a useful spot for washing clothes, rinsing tools, and playing. But Harper's Brook offered danger as well. Few people in Brigstock could swim well, so if a young girl lost her footing or a man tumbled down the bank, she or he was likely to drown.

Beyond the fields and assarts of Brigstock lay a place just as dangerous and productive as Harper's Brook: the forest. Some parts of the forest were heavily wooded, but other sections lay open for pasture or other uses. To Cecilia and her family, the wooded parts of the forest were a frightening place where outlaws, fairies, and other unknowns might be encountered. Perhaps they told stories, as did later generations, of a disastrous visit by the forest outlaw Robin Hood to Brigstock. The tale relates how Robin and his men, attacked while in church, made a bold escape, but left behind a dead priest, inadvertently stuck by an arrow while celebrating mass. Despite the many dangers—human and supernatural—of the forest, the Penifaders went into it often, for it was an important part of their economy of makeshifts. With her mother and siblings, young Cecilia gathered fallen wood in the forest; helped in the digging of peat; checked on the Penifader pigs feeding wild in the underbrush; and collected nuts, berries, honey, and herbs. Whenever her father or brothers had the nerve, they probably also trapped hare and shot deer in the forest. If caught by foresters, they would have been prosecuted for *poaching* because animals on royal preserves were to be hunted only by the king or his friends, and if convicted of poaching, peasants usually faced fines or imprisonment.

---

[5]Cultivation of new lands played a critical role in the history of the medieval rural economy. Between 1000 and 1300, peasants brought thousands of acres of previously untilled land—marshes, wasteland, moors, and unpopulated territories—into cultivation. Often this was small scale, as with assarts. But sometimes, it was large scale, with lords attracting settlers to new, previously uncultivated lands. Perhaps this sort of large-scale settlement explains the founding of Stanion by settlers from Brigstock, but the date of Stanion's settlement and its causes are unknown. In any case, large-scale colonization was especially important on the European continent. From the eleventh century, for example, vast areas east of the Elbe were settled by peasants drawn by lords offering attractive rents and terms. Whether by small assarts or large-scale colonization, the hard work of peasants bringing new lands under the plow was the basic means of economic expansion in the later medieval countryside. After 1100, peasants had few new technologies with which to improve their productivity, but they could, and did, bring new lands into cultivation.

So when Cecilia ventured outside her parents' house and farmyard, she walked among a tight cluster of homes in Stanion, crowded on a few streets. She found the same whenever she wandered down Harper's Brook to Brigstock village. Surrounding these two clusters of houses and outbuildings, lay arable fields, meadows, pastures, and forest, and in all of these, Cecilia would have worked and played as a young child. She would have gone into the fields often to help with weeding, breaking clods of earth, tying bundles at harvest, or perhaps even moving ever so slightly the boundary stones that separated Penifader and Everard land; in the pastures around Brigstock, she watched animals or drove them to and from various fields; she played and fished in Harper's Brook; and she accompanied her mother into the forest to forage for nuts, berries, fallen wood, and other necessities. This was the Brigstock and Stanion that Cecilia knew, within about 7,600 acres lay two nucleated settlements of about nine hundred adults, several arable fields, extensive pasture and meadow, numerous small assarts, a stream full of fish, and a forest beyond.

THE WIDER WORLD

Cecilia's world did not end at the boundaries of Brigstock and Stanion. As a child, she would often have run into the street to stare at people passing through—pilgrims on their way to holy shrines; knights and ladies riding out for pleasure or hunting; peddlers offering goods for sale; carpenters and thatchers looking for work; beggars seeking alms; migrant laborers following the harvest; even other peasants walking through Brigstock on their way to the weekly markets held in nearby villages and towns. Some of these people stopped for a while in Brigstock, perhaps to visit with kin or perhaps to take

Brigstock and its region.

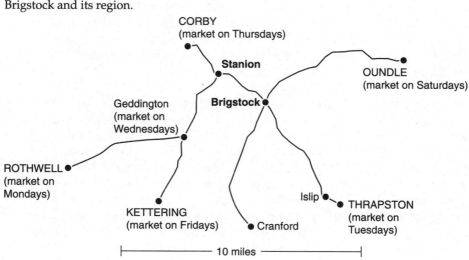

advantage of some occasional employment. Some even ended up settling in the community. Over the course of Cecilia's life, about one-third of the people in Brigstock came from elsewhere to settle on the manor (and a roughly equal proportion left Brigstock to seek their fortunes elsewhere). Whether staying for a long or short time, these newcomers brought news and gossip of other places, new ideas, new fashions, new songs. From them, Cecilia learned early that there were villages, towns, and people far beyond what she saw with her own eyes.

Moreover, as she grew older, Cecilia saw many more people and places. Most peasants moved readily and often within a fifteen-mile radius of the villages in which they lived and worked. Brigstock was especially well situated, surrounded by nearby towns or villages, all within ten miles or less, that hosted markets on one day of every week. On any day, except Sunday, the Penifaders could easily reach a market—Rothwell on Monday, Thrapston on Tuesday, Geddington on Wednesday, Corby on Thursday, Kettering on Friday, and Oundle on Saturday. At these markets, the Penifaders bought and sold goods; hired workers and offered themselves for hire; gossiped about Brigstock news; and heard stories from other places. They traveled by foot, walking with an ease and speed that many hikers today might envy. At a pace of about four miles an hour, Cecilia's mother could reach Corby in two hours, sell her eggs and cheese, and get back home well before dark. At the same pace, her father could get to Kettering market on a Friday, collect a new plowshare, and return within one day, and her sister Christina could walk to the village of Cranford, spend an afternoon with the man she eventually married, and be home for supper. By the time Cecilia reached the age of eight, she was probably accompanying her parents and older siblings on trips such as these. From then on, she was well aware of the world beyond the village of her birth. She talked with itinerant peddlers and laborers, she sold and bought goods at local markets, and she visited her married sister in Cranford.

Cecilia seems to have never left Brigstock for an extended period, but one of her brothers did; to get an education, William Penifader left his home for almost a decade, and when he returned to Brigstock, he brought the sophistication of a man who had walked the streets of such towns as Oxford, Cambridge, Lincoln, or possibly, London. Perhaps Cecilia also traveled a bit, and if so, she most likely undertook a pilgrimage to Lincoln, about sixty miles to the north. There, pilgrims prayed at the shrine of Little St. Hugh, a boy supposedly martyred by the Jews in 1255. When Hugh's body was discovered in a well, hysterical townspeople accused eighteen Jews of his murder and hanged them; such accusations, known as 'blood libel' accusations, first developed in twelfth-century Europe, but they soon became a common and dangerous expression of Christian anti-Semitism. At York in 1190, for example, 150 Jews—men, women, and children—were massacred after another spurious charge of child murder. For Cecilia, however, Hugh of Lincoln was not an unfortunate child whose death was explained away by false charges against Jews; he was a holy martyr whose cult attracted attention far and wide. If she did journey to Lincoln to pray at his shrine, her pilgrimage combined piety and pleasure.

Like the pilgrims of Chaucer's *Canterbury Tales,* she would have met new people, seen new places, and learned new customs and ideas.

Cecilia was further integrated into a wider world by the bureaucracy of the English realm. By the late thirteenth century, English kings offered justice to their subjects in a variety of forums including hundred courts, county courts, courts in Westminster, and most importantly, courts convened by itinerant justices. Most of the crimes and quarrels of Brigstock were easily resolved in its three-weekly manorial court, but some crimes could only be adjudicated in royal courts. Any untimely death, for example, had to be investigated by the king's coroner, and any accused murderers could only be tried before the king's justices. The exchequer, the heart of the royal finances, also reached into the lives of Cecilia and other people in Brigstock. When the king's officers arrived to collect taxes, they expected cooperation from local deputies and prompt payment by local taxpayers. And the military demands of England's kings also touched the lives of ordinary peasants, expected to contribute men and supplies to the army. As a woman, Cecilia never had to testify on a royal **jury** or serve in the king's army, but she knew well the power and strength of the king's courts, his exchequer, and his army.

Cecilia met few foreigners. Living as she did in the heart of the English midlands, she might never have encountered anyone from Wales, Scotland, France, or even farther afield. She almost certainly never met a non-Christian, for few Muslims traveled to medieval England and Jews had been expelled from England in 1290. Yet Cecilia lived in a multilingual culture. Lords and ladies spoke French; all clerics and clerks knew some Latin; and every parishioner was familiar with the Latin mass, celebrated every Sunday and on other holy days, too. Cecilia's mother tongue was English, but she possibly understood a few words or phrases in French and Latin. All in all, Cecilia's horizons might not have been as broad as those of most modern people, but she knew a great deal about the world that lay beyond the fields of Brigstock and Stanion.

SUGGESTIONS FOR FURTHER READING

For essays on rural settlement, agricultural tools, and human use of the land, see Grenville Astill and Annie Grant, ed., *The Countryside of Medieval England* (1988) and Leonard Cantor, *The English Medieval Landscape* (1982). For colonization, see Robert Bartlett, *The Making of Europe: Conquest, Colonization, and Cultural Change, 950–1350* (1993). For a fascinating look at what modern archaeological excavations have revealed about peasant life in the Middle Ages, see Maurice Beresford and John Hurst, *Wharram Percy: Deserted Medieval Village* (1990). See also the essays on specific aspects of rural settlement and economy in Christopher Dyer, *Everyday Life in Medieval England* (1994).

General information about Brigstock during Cecilia's day can be found in my *Women in the Medieval English Countryside: Gender and Household in Brigstock Before the Plague* (1987).

CHAPTER 3

Lords, Ladies, and Peasants

On a chilly afternoon in December 1290, Robert and Alice Penifader probably put aside their work and walked about three miles southwest to the village of Geddington. There, they saw a grieving king: Edward I escorting the body of his queen, Eleanor of Castile, from Lincoln to London. The cortege stayed in Geddington overnight. In later years, the Penifaders would have remembered this sad procession whenever they visited Geddington, for Edward I ordered that crosses be erected at each of the twelve sites where Eleanor's body had rested for a night. Cecilia was not born when this grim procession moved so close to her home, but as a small child, she might have played at the foot of this "Eleanor Cross" whenever her parents took her to Geddington for the Wednesday market. Children do the same today. Most of the Eleanor Crosses are gone, but the one in Geddington is the best preserved of the three that remain.[1]

As they stood in Geddington on that cold evening in 1290, Robert and Alice Penifader got as close as they ever would to a king and queen of England. Like all peasants, they were taught to revere royalty, and Edward I, an especially strong and bellicose king, inspired special respect. He had faced baronial revolt in his youth, but in 1290, such threats were in the past. Ruling by the fact of his birth, the power of his wealth, the influence of his bureaucracy, the force of his personality, and the success of his military campaigns, Edward I was a formidable figure. For Robert and Alice Penifader, however, Edward I was even more than an awesome king, far richer and more powerful than anyone else in their world. He was also their manorial lord.

[1]The most famous Eleanor Cross stands outside (and gave its name to) Charing Cross Station in London, but this cross is a nineteenth-century reconstruction.

The Eleanor Cross in the village of Geddington, as it
appears today.

Brigstock was a royal manor. Sometimes the king took the profits of the
manor for himself, but usually he granted it to his queen as part of her *dower*
(that is, as part of the lands designated for her support in widowhood).[2] In
1262, Brigstock had been assigned to the mother of Edward I, Eleanor of

[2]Dower and **dowry** are often confused, but they were different things. Dower consisted of a por-
tion (usually one-third) of a deceased husband's lands that a widow could use until her death.
Dower was often specified at the time of marriage so that everyone would know, if the husband
died first, what his widow's rightful claims would be. Dowry consisted of cash, goods, or properties that a bride's family gave to the new couple at the time of marriage. Sometimes the dowry returned to the wife if her husband predeceased her. Both dower and dowry could provide support
for widows, but they came from different sources. The use of dower or dowry shifted over time,
but by Cecilia's day, dower was more common in England and northern Europe, and dowry was
more common in southern Europe.

Provence; after her death in 1292, the manor passed to Edward I; then to his second wife Margaret of France; then to Edward II; and finally to *his* wife Isabella of France (who died in 1358). As these transfers suggest, royal revenues were a complex business, and Brigstock manor was just a tiny piece of the pie (in 1262, for example, it accounted for only 1 percent of Eleanor of Provence's dower). No royal lord or lady of Brigstock seems to have ever visited the manor, and, indeed, they usually leased it out. Under such agreements, the lessee of Brigstock managed the manor, paying an agreed-upon sum each year to the king or queen in whose possession it then resided. For the Penifaders, the seignorial power of the manor's royal owners was a distant power.

Of the three institutions that structured life in Brigstock—village, parish, and manor—the last was the most removed from the day-to-day life of Cecilia Penifader. Every day she chatted with some neighbors, worked with others, and fed her sheep on the fields and pastures that were open, by general agreement and custom, to common use. She sometimes argued with her neighbors and sometimes stole from them too, but for her, the "community of the vill" was a real community. The parish also wielded a strong presence in Cecilia's life. The churches of St. Andrew and St. Peter were the most imposing buildings around; the priests, one of whom was likely Cecilia's brother, probably impressed everyone with their education, religious authority, and perhaps also, sanctity; and the masses said by these priests attracted Cecilia to church not only on Sundays but also on many holy days throughout the year. The manor of Brigstock was also important to Cecilia, for she paid her rents to the manor and brought her business before its court. But the manor was a more extraneous entity. Devised as a profit-making mechanism for its owners, Brigstock manor was part of a grid for the management of land and people that had been superimposed, many centuries before Cecilia's day, on the already settled villages of the English midlands. In the case of Brigstock, as we have seen, this grid had settled messily on the village, for Brigstock manor excluded a few small holdings in the village of Brigstock and took in much of nearby Stanion as well as small bits of two other nearby villages. Brigstock manor made its small contribution to the revenues of its lord or lady in typical ways: the produce from the demesne, the rents of the tenants, and the income generated by court fines and administrative fees. In Eleanor of Provence's day, she and her clerks knew precisely how much money they could expect to get out of Brigstock each year: £41 and 10 shillings.[3] Small as this was in the context of royal finances, £41 and 10 shillings was a lot of money to the peasants of Brigstock: it amounted to more than 6,500 days of work, if calculated at the wages then earned by a man who hired himself out for ordinary day labor.

---

[3]The symbol £ designates a **pound sterling.** In the monetary system then used, a penny was the basic coin, a **shilling** consisted of 12 **pence,** and there were 20 shillings (or 240 pence) to the pound sterling.

SEIGNORIAL POWERS

Compared to most medieval peasants, Cecilia Penifader and the other tenants of Brigstock were remarkably unencumbered by manorialism, that is, somewhat removed from the system of estates through which the landed elite profited from "those who work." Cecilia and her neighbors never saw the owners of their manor; they did not suffer from over-zealous administrators; they enjoyed an especially privileged legal status; and they were even able, for most of Cecilia's life, to manage Brigstock manor on their own.

Cecilia grew up, reached maturity, aged, sickened, and died without ever bowing before any lord or lady of Brigstock. Yet most peasants lived in much closer proximity to their lords or ladies, especially if their manors were held by petty baronial or knightly families (that is, the *gentry*). Holding only a few manors or even just one, these knights and ladies often lived on their manors for at least part of the year. Sometimes they traveled from manor to manor, consuming the produce of each demesne before they moved on. Resident lords and ladies exerted a powerful and continuing presence over the lives of tenants. They required deference at all times—a bowed head when met in the street, a special place in the parish church, an immediate response to any request or command. They proffered hospitality, especially at Christmas, when it was customary to open the hall of the manor house to feasting by the tenants. And they sometimes directly managed the manor, supervising the tenancies; presiding over the manorial court; and taking its profitable rents, fines, and fees. Resident lords and ladies knew their tenants well, and their tenants probably knew them even better. This sort of intimate seignorial relationship was far from the experience of the people of Brigstock. William I and Henry I each visited Brigstock briefly, but when the newly widowed Edward I stopped in Geddington on that cold evening in December 1290, he got as close to Brigstock as would any of the kings of the thirteenth or fourteenth centuries.

Many medieval peasants also endured much closer administrative supervision than did the tenants of Brigstock, especially if their manors were part of an ecclesiastical estate. Manors could be held by institutions as well as by people, and many monasteries, colleges, and bishoprics developed highly sophisticated mechanisms for administering their various lands and tenants. The abbey of Ramsey, for example, held twenty-three manors in the region to the east and south of Brigstock, and its officers were constantly moving between these manors—keeping accounts, checking on reeves (the men responsible for most of the day-to-day work of the manor), convening courts, and generally making sure that everything was managed as efficiently and as profitably as possible. Armed with ink and parchment, these clerks kept such careful records that they could trace persons, lands, and money owed across many generations. For medieval peasants, clerical literacy often translated into seignorial power. Documents that most peasants could not read might seal their fate: whether they were free or serf; whether they could or could not inherit some land from their parents; whether their rents could or could not be raised. Whenever peasants rose in revolt, they sought these documents—sometimes to burn them and sometimes in the hope that they guaranteed privileges unjustly denied. Cecilia and her neighbors were somewhat insulated from the seignorial power of parchment and ink. More often than not, supervision and recordkeeping in Brigstock was of the tenants' own making. Since they were usually able to lease Brigstock manor themselves, they selected, directed, and paid the clerks who recorded the business of court meetings and who kept the accounts.

Perhaps most important, many medieval peasants were personally unfree in ways that the Penifaders and other tenants of Brigstock were not. A free peasant was able to emigrate, work, marry, and take grievances to the king's court; a serf was restricted in all these respects. There were many intermediate categories between freedom and serfdom, and to complicate matters even more, these distinctions were applied to land as well as people (so that a free woman might hold land for which the labor services of serfdom were due). By Cecilia's time, serfdom meant less than it once had, but it was still onerous enough that peasants sought to evade or escape it whenever possible.

Serfs differed from free peasants in three important ways. First, serfs were "tied to the land," and if they wished to marry someone on another manor or move elsewhere, they had to get permission to do so. Many serfs never moved away from the manors of their birth. Of those who did, some left surreptitiously, but most paid a small annual fee (called **chevage**) to live legally off the manor. They paid the fee, doubtless grudgingly, because it thereby assured not only that they could return for visits but also that no one else, especially their parents, would suffer for their unauthorized absence. This was a heavy enough burden, but the second burden was worse: serfs had to pay some of

Boon-work during harvest. As a reeve directs, men reap the demesne. Peasants deeply resented boon-work, because it took them away from their own fields at a particularly critical time of the year.

Carting. Three men push a cart while the driver urges on the horses. Carting was part of the manorial labor required from serfs, and it was dangerous work. Men often died under the wheels of carts or the hooves of horses.

their rent in labor. Many had to do **week-work** on demesne lands, usually a day or two each week spent plowing, sowing, weeding, or doing whatever the reeve said needed to be done; almost all had to do **boon-works** during harvest, that is, they had to undertake special work harvesting crops on the demesne (in compensation for their extra work during harvest, serfs often got food and ale); and some others were also obliged to perform other petty services, such as carting or carrying goods at certain times to certain places.

Third, serfs often had to pay a variety of small fines and fees, which were expensive, irritating, and, in some cases, humiliating. Many manors required serfs to use manorial services—mills, winepresses, ovens—whose profits went, of course, into the hands of the lord or lady. Often peasants tried to avoid these expenses (for example, by using handmills to grind their own grain or seeking out millers who charged cheap prices), but many lords and ladies obstructed these money-saving strategies by insisting that *their* serfs had to patronize *their* mills, winepresses, and ovens. Another small fee was the **leyrwite,** due from any young women, and sometimes young men, who were sexually active before marriage. Marriage itself could be costly; unfree women often had to pay **merchet,** due for permission to marry. Most manors also required that a **heriot** be paid whenever a tenant died. Traditionally, the heriot was the most valuable animal of the dead tenant, but this was often converted to a cash amount. Finally, on many manors, lords and ladies enjoyed the right of **tallage,** the right to levy an arbitrary tax on serfs. Heriot and tallage sprang from the same fundamental principle: the notion that all of a serf's property, movable goods as well as tenancies, ultimately belonged to the lord or lady. Everything a serf possessed—cash, furniture, clothing, pots, bedding, sheep, pigs, goats, and land—was held "at the will of" the manorial lord or lady.

These obligations of serfdom were costly and demeaning. Of them all, serfs especially resented obligatory work, for days spent laboring on the demesne were days lost from work on their own tenancies. They also strongly resented the uncertainty of their obligations. A lord or lady might levy tallage in one year and not the next, or might convert labor services into cash payments in one year and insist on their performance in the next; these legitimate but arbitrary actions introduced a maddening instability into peasant budgets. Whenever they could, serfs aggressively and persistently sought freedom. They tried to avoid paying servile fees such as merchet or tallage; they purchased their freedom; they went to court to claim free descent; and especially in the decades that followed the Black Death of 1347–9, they rebelled against the manorial regime.

Distinctions between free and unfree readily capture modern imaginations, and it would certainly be a mistake to underestimate serfdom. But it would also be a mistake to make too much of distinctions between free peasants and serfs. After all, free peasants had obligations too. They had to pay their rents, render deference to their "social betters," answer charges in manorial courts, and sometimes even take business to manorial mills or other facilities. Moreover, although distinctions between free and unfree were important, they did not mean as much by 1300 as they had in the past. It helped a bit that some obligations of serfs were set by *custom* and could not be changed for the worse. Whatever a serf's parents had done, he or she also had to do—but no more. In fact, custom sometimes protected serfs from market forces. In the late thirteenth century, as population pressure made land scarce and more valuable, rents on free lands were readily raised to new highs, but rents on serf lands stayed at their old, customary levels. Serfs were similarly protected by rules, found on many manors, against the subdivision of unfree tenements. Free tenants so often divided their lands between sons that after a few generations, many free tenants held small, even tiny, properties. Serfs, sometimes required to keep tenancies intact by lords or ladies who wanted easy-to-collect rents, had to provide for noninheriting children in other ways. As a result, some serfs numbered among the prosperous few who held thirty acres or more, while many free tenants possessed holdings that were too small to support their households. In other words, serfdom was an undesirable state, but it would be wrong to equate serfdom with poverty and degradation. By Cecilia's time, free and unfree peasants regularly intermarried, held each other's lands, and otherwise intermingled. Although freedom and serfdom still determined various rents and obligations, the lines were so blurred and confused that they had fairly weak social meaning. In most villages by 1300, it mattered more whether you held thirty acres or five acres than whether you were free or unfree.

In any case, distinctions of free and unfree were even less relevant to the people of Brigstock. Like many other manors in royal forests, Brigstock was part of the **ancient demesne,** defined as the manors held directly by William the Conqueror at the time of the Domesday Survey in 1086. Long before Cecilia's birth, tenants of the ancient demesne had come to enjoy a special legal status, different from either free peasants or serfs: lawyers called them "privileged villeins of the ancient demesne." Cecilia and her fellow tenants had to tolerate a few vestigial remnants of serfdom: they had to pay various small annual fees; they had to provide minimal labor services (especially boon-works at harvest); their tenancies had to pass through the bailiff's hands whenever sold, transferred, or inherited; and they had, in a few restricted instances, to pay merchet and heriot. But the tenants of Brigstock and other ancient demesne manors had privileges unknown to other peasants, either free or serf: they did not have to pay tolls or customs anywhere in England; they could not be obliged to attend county courts; and they were able to use royal writs to bring their cases to court (this meant that they could use the power of the king to resolve disputes, especially property disputes, in their favor). Cecilia's status, then, exemplifies the blurring between free and unfree that was so common by her time. Neither a freewoman nor a serf, she tolerated a few servile obligations but also enjoyed other exceptional privileges.

The most startling manifestation of Brigstock's unusual manorial status was the leasing of the manor by its tenants. Under this arrangement, the people of Brigstock managed their own manor. They took profits off the demesne by cultivating it or renting it out; they convened the court and made sure that its fines were paid; they collected all rents and fees. From these profits, they paid the lease of the manor, and as long as they paid the lease on time, they were left alone until the lease expired. The privilege of leasing their manor was dearly bought by the tenants of Brigstock. In 1270, they purchased a ten-year lease at a one-time cost of more than £13, promising further that they would pay an extra 30 shillings per year beyond the manor's set value. In 1318, the tenants offered the king £50 each year to lease directly from him, but he refused and instead, probably as a favor, offered the lease to Margery de Farendraght for about £13 a year. The tenants then promised to pay £46 annually to sublease the manor from her. Dearly bought, the privilege of managing their own manorial regime must have been much valued by the people of Brigstock.

Why was this privilege so highly valued? After all, when the tenants held the lease or sublease of Brigstock manor, they were not free of the rents, fines, fees, and services they had owed to Eleanor of Provence when her officers administered the manor directly. These obligations were as necessary as ever, for they generated the income needed to pay the lease. Yet, as the tenants of Brigstock charged themselves to raise the money for their lease, they gained two tangible benefits. First, they gained some dignity. Like townspeople who were often fiercely proud of the charters whereby they acquired some rights of self-government, the people of Brigstock rightly valued the privilege of managing their manor themselves.[4] Cecilia and her neighbors still had to defer to their "social betters," but they ensured, for the duration of the lease, that no one might demand special dues as lord or lady of Brigstock and no one might try to revive old obligations or impose new ones. Second and perhaps more important, they gained some economic relief and some stability of obligation. Since the tenants managed the profit-making capabilities of Brigstock manor with the sole purpose of paying the lease, they were not interested in profit for profit's sake. Once the lease was paid, there was no need to milk manorial perquisites for every possible penny. Whenever the manor lay in the hands of the tenants themselves, in other words, the people of Brigstock could rest easier about their tenancies and goods. They paid what they had to pay to cover the lease, but no more.

As the leasing of Brigstock manor to its tenants shows, profit-taking was at the heart of the manorial enterprise. To be sure, seignorial rights spoke to the inferiority of tenants and the deference expected from them. A merchet generated income, but it also symbolized the dependency of serfs who could not marry without permission. Week-work was important for cultivating the demesne, but it also spoke to the inability of serfs to control their own labor and time. To be sure, the dominating power of the feudal elite also ensured that peasants did what they were supposed to do. So far as peasants paid merchets and performed week-work, they did so because they would incur fines, punishments, and other unpleasantness if they did not respect their "social betters." Dependency and domination were, therefore, critical to manorialism, but they were supporting actors to the main manorial role: profit. For many peasants, the people of Brigstock among them, seignorial power was expressed more often through clerks, officers, and administrators than through the imposing presence of a resident lord or lady.

PEASANTS AND THEIR "SOCIAL BETTERS"

During the harvest of 1304, two of Cecilia's sisters, Emma and Alice, failed to appear for boon-works on the demesne, and that September they were cited in court because they had "refused to do the boon-work of our lord the king." How should we understand their absence? It is possible that the Penifaders forgot to bring everyone to the boon-work, leaving behind their least fit children (both girls seem to have died at early ages). But it is also possible that the absence of Emma and Alice from this servile labor was deliberate, a small but telling way in which the Penifaders resisted the seignorial power of Brigstock's lord. Just as we cannot know whether the absence of Emma and Alice Penifader from one harvest boon-work in 1304 was accident or deliberate de-

---

[4]In a sense, the leasing of manors by tenants was much like the arrangements whereby medieval towns were allowed to be self-governing for the payment of an annual "fee-farm." The main difference was that a manorial lease expired after a set term of years, whereas a town's fee-farm extended forever unless revoked for some extraordinary cause.

sign, so we cannot know about the many other instances in which tenants fell foul of their servile obligations. Was a missed week-work a matter of forgetfulness or resistance? Were unpaid rents a matter of poverty or truculence? Was a marriage concluded without merchet a clever dodge to save money or a deliberate assertion of the right to marry without seignorial permission?

While we cannot always know how to interpret instances in which peasants failed to fulfill manorial obligations, we can be certain of several things about relations between peasants, on the one hand, and the lords or ladies of manors, on the other. First, tenants often came up short in meeting their obligations. Work was left unfinished; rents and fines were unpaid; and other things got done only after repeated reminders and even harassment. Second, tenants sometimes fulfilled their duties in sullen and minimal ways. For example, reeves complained long and hard about the unenthusiastic efforts of serfs forced to work on the demesne: they came late to work; they paid poor attention to instructions; they worked slowly. Third, tenants occasionally resisted seignorial demands outright. Some serfs on a Ramsey manor to the southeast of Brigstock got so angry about the poor quality of food provided at their boon-works that they walked off and refused to work. One young man on another Ramsey manor resisted forced boon-works in a surprisingly modern way—he lay down in the field, obstructing with his body further work on the harvest. Other tenants argued with their lords or ladies over more substantial matters such as new increases in labor services, and, in some cases, these disputes dragged on for years and even ended up before the justices of the king. One famous case pitted the tenants of Halesowen, located about 60 miles west of Brigstock, against the abbey that held the manor. It lasted for more than seventy years, and involved royal inquests, petitions to the king's council, settlements gone awry, and a great deal of animosity. In the end, the abbey won.

After the Black Death of 1347–9, resistance to manorialism took a new turn, with peasants mounting full-scale revolts to better their circumstances. The first revolt was the French *Jacquerie* of 1358 (so called because many peasant men in France were named Jacques). In England, the Peasants' Revolt in 1381 severely frightened the landowning elite, and Jack Cade's Rebellion in 1450 did much the same. In Germany, peasants sought, in the Peasants' War of 1524–5, to ease some of their social and economic difficulties. In all these cases, peasants were cruelly crushed by the forces of the feudal elite. Yet they often won in the long haul, for many of their demands were eventually met, albeit slowly. For example, the English peasants of 1381 sought, among other things, the abolition of serfdom. To this end, rebels burned buildings, murdered several people (including the Archbishop of Canterbury), and marched on London. There, they met on two occasions with the fourteen-year-old Richard II. The rebels revered the king and trusted him; their anger was aimed at the lords and ladies of their own manors—that is, at those who demanded their labor services, collected their rents, and gave, the peasants thought, bad advice to a good king. When the peasant leader Wat Tyler was slain in the second meeting and Richard II asked the crowds to disperse, the rebels left

London. From that point on, their revolt was doomed; they were hunted down, imprisoned, and hanged. Serfdom was not abolished. But within a hundred years, it had almost withered away in England—thanks in part to peasant resistance, but thanks also to new economic circumstances that changed the ways in which lords and ladies tried to profit from their manors. The rebels of 1381 lost, but their descendants eventually won.

For the people of Brigstock in the early fourteenth century, tensions over seignorial demands were less intense than elsewhere, if only because seignorial demands were relatively mild. Indeed, in their suit against the abbey, the tenants of Halesowen sought to be treated as privileged villeins of the ancient demesne; they sought the status that Cecilia and others in Brigstock already enjoyed. On a scale that extended from the most oppressed of medieval serfs to those peasants least restricted by manorialism, Cecilia and the other tenants of Brigstock would be placed toward the least restricted end. Yet this does not mean that Cecilia was free of seignorial demands and servile obligations; it means that she lived under a muted form of manorialism. Moreover, manorialism was just one aspect of Cecilia's subservient place. Like all medieval peasants, Cecilia lived under the ever-present shadow of superior powers, of which the power of the lord or lady of Brigstock was but one. Cecilia was, after all, a mere peasant in a world where peasants were humble people.

As a child, Cecilia learned from the clergy—her parish priest, his assistants, or perhaps the sermons of visiting friars—to see the world as divided into three mutually supporting groups or orders. This tripartite view of medieval society was discussed in chapter 1. Developed by clerical authors in the eleventh century, it had been popularized by Cecilia's day, and it was commonly taken to represent God's will for the ordering of human relations. The first and most important was the clerical order, composed of "those who pray." By their prayers and holy service, bishops, priests, monks, nuns, and friars bridged the gap between ordinary people and God. Since Cecilia had been taught that the business of life was eternal salvation, it was probably easy to convince her that the holy efforts of "those who pray" were much more important than her own modest work on the land. Moreover, without the priests who managed the two churches of Brigstock and the friars who preached sermons when they passed through Brigstock, Cecilia's life would have been much more boring and dull. As we shall see in chapter 4, Christianity, with its crowded calendar of festivals and rituals, created a steady rhythm of worship, celebration, and festivity that richly shaped the days and years of Cecilia's life.

Second in importance came the landed elite, "those who fight." By their military power and strong governance, kings, earls, barons, and knights ensured, according to the theory, that everyone else could go about their business in peace and security. Unlike peasants elsewhere, Cecilia did not have to seek much protection from war and invasion. If she had lived in Spain (where Christian armies of the *Reconquista* were pushing back Islamic settlement) or on the western borders of the Holy Roman Empire (where threats from Slavs, Mongols, and others loomed large), she might have been especially grateful to feudal armies that protected villages from destruction and, in some cases, won new lands for settlement. Yet even Cecilia, living in the relatively stable and secure English midlands, could be grateful for strong knights and strong kings. These men brought peace to her countryside; they discouraged marauders and bandits; and they punished those guilty of murder, theft, rape, and other felonies. Cecilia probably readily believed that the firm hand of Edward I was a hand that protected her, not only from Welsh and Scots invaders but also from murderers, rapists, and other felons. Third, at the bottom of the heap came the mass of medieval peasants, "those who work." By the sweat of her hard labor, Cecilia supported, so priests and friars taught her, those who prayed for her soul and guaranteed her security.

This was a neat and coherent theory. Every order had a role to play, and if each did its part well, salvation, security, and support were assured. But this theory worked less well in practice. To begin with, some groups of people fit poorly into the theory. As Cecilia might have considered whenever she walked or rode a cart to the towns of Northampton or Peterborough, there was really no place in this tripartite world for merchants, artisans, and other townspeople. She might also have wondered about where women fit in. The tripartite scheme dwelt little on women's roles and sometimes even accommodated women as a "fourth estate," separate from and beneath the three estates of male clergy, male warriors, and male peasants. Moreover, the theory was too idealized. As Cecilia also might have often observed, clerics could sin with as much gusto as they prayed, and they were sometimes more noted for their wealth than for their holiness. Similarly, she learned that the feudal elite could cause disorder as well as peace. Violent and proud, these men, and sometimes women, thought nothing of pursuing petty arguments through battle, cantering through ripening fields in pursuit of deer, or breaking fences and scattering herds that stood in their way. Most of all, Cecilia likely felt, when tithes, taxes, and rents were all due at once, that her role as a woman among "those who work" was the hardest and least fulfilling of the three.

Alongside this idyllic but not entirely convincing tripartite scheme of three mutually supportive orders was another worldview, one that saw a straightforward division between privileged and not-privileged, empowered and disempowered. On one side stood elites; on the other side stood ordinary people. On one side stood barons, nuns, merchants, and many people even richer and more powerful; on the other side stood laborers, peasants, and the poor. This was the world view that English peasants rejected a few generations after Cecilia's death when, in the Peasants' Revolt of 1381, they asked:

> *When Adam delved and Eve span,*
> *Who then was a gentleman?*

What was the biblical justification, they were asking, for dividing people into "haves" and "have-nots"? This radical question, phrased in exactly this form, was raised by disgruntled peasants throughout Europe on many occasions between 1300 and 1550.

Both views of medieval society—the tripartite view, which ranked peasants last, and the bipartite view, which separated the privileged and the not-privileged—encouraged elites to see themselves as better sorts of people, almost different races. They treated peasants with scorn and disgust, and they described peasants as dishonest, irreligious, dirty, stupid drudges. Said to be descended from Cain or Ham, peasants were seen as almost a different race made for sweated work alone. "What should a serf do," asked one monk, "but serve?" Perhaps the most startling manifestation of elite disdain for the peasantry is the ready assumption by privileged men that peasant women were theirs for the taking. Sometimes peasants were seen as so naturally lascivious that men could easily, as one text for young scholars put it, "make free with their wives and daughters." Sometimes peasant women were seen as natural prey for elite men. Courtly poems written in the twelfth and thirteenth centuries celebrated the rape of peasant women by young knights, and Andreas Capellanus, the twelfth-century author of *The Art of Courtly Love*, advised any knight enamored of an unyielding peasant maiden, "do not hesitate to take what you seek and to embrace her by force."[5] Rape cases were rarely prosecuted in medieval courts, so we cannot know how often this talk about the sexual availability of peasant women was translated into action. As best we know, Cecilia never fell victim to such deluded ideas.

Because Cecilia was a mere peasant, there were many things that she could not do. Peasants were often pious, but they seldom found careers in the Church. Precocious boys like her brother William occasionally took holy orders and served in rural parishes, but there were almost no peasant monks or nuns, no peasant bishops (Robert Grosseteste is the exception) or popes, and indeed, few peasant saints. Peasants were often clever, but most received no formal education, and even those few seldom advanced to training at universities or law courts. Peasants were sometimes wealthy, but they rarely found merchants or knights willing to deal with them as business partners, or, even more unlikely, willing to join their families in marriage. Peasants were often politically astute, but when Edward I began to call together the first parliaments of England, he gathered lords, churchmen, knights, and townsmen into Westminster Hall, but not a single peasant. Peasants were the pariahs of the medieval world. They were sometimes pitied for their poverty, but neither their persons nor their labors were appreciated by others. Peasants far outnumbered the ecclesiastical, feudal, and mercantile elites, but the wealth and power of the Middle Ages lay beyond their reach.

Within the community of Brigstock, Cecilia was born into a well-off and well-respected family. By the standards of most medieval peasants, her lot was an enviable one indeed. Yet Cecilia's life was structured at every turn by people and institutions more powerful than she. The Church told her how she

---

[5]Many people today think that manorial lords also had the "right of first night," that is, the right to have sexual intercourse with a newly married serf before she slept with her husband. This idea, critical to the plots of the opera *The Marriage of Figaro* and the movie *Braveheart*, is a fabrication of some sixteenth-century imaginations. Manorial lords had many powers, but they did not include the systematic and legal rape of female serfs.

should live and worship; it stood ready to punish her if need arose; and it took a compulsory tithe from her fields and flocks. The king claimed the right to punish her for murder, theft, and other major crimes, and to collect, when he had need, taxes, food, and men from Cecilia and the other tenants of Brigstock. The king and queen also sought, as lord and lady of Brigstock, to take as much profit from Brigstock manor, by lease or direct management, as they could. And any merchant, knight, or abbess who rode through Brigstock expected Cecilia to greet them with proper deference and humility. Well-off within her community, Cecilia was just another peasant to the many different sorts of people who sought to profit from her life and labor. It is easy to understand the powers of these people and to describe them, but it is impossible to answer the most intriguing question: What did Cecilia think about it? When she bowed to a passing lady, paid rent to the Queen's bailiff, or bargained with a merchant, did she think that her "social betters" were truly better than she?

SUGGESTIONS FOR FURTHER READING

Relations between English landowners and peasants came to a head in the Peasant's Revolt of 1381. Rodney Hilton's study of that revolt, *Bond Men Made Free: Medieval Peasant Movements and the English Rising of 1381* (1973), provides an excellent introduction to the subject. See also Hilton's *The Decline of Serfdom in Medieval England* (1969). For an interesting and complicated debate among historians about the importance of seignorial demands in late medieval Europe, see T. H. Aston and C. H. E. Philpin, eds., *The Brenner Debate: Agrarian Class Structure and Economic Development in Pre-Industrial Europe* (1985). See also Guy Fourquin, *Lordship and Feudalism in the Middle Ages* (1976).

For the rape of rural women, see Kathryn Gravdal's *Ravishing Maidens: Writing Rape in Medieval French Literature and Law* (1991).

CHAPTER 4

Parish, Belief, Ritual

In July 1326, Cecilia's brother William went to the Brigstock court and arranged to have his lands inherited by a young man identified as John, the son of Alice Perse of Kingsthorpe. William's grant specified twenty separate properties, including his own house in Stanion, located next door to the house of his sister Cecilia. Almost twenty years later, John again appeared in the Brigstock court, this time to argue about the inheritance of Cecilia Penifader. He lost this argument, but in the course of it, he was identified as Cecilia's nephew. In other words, John, the son of Alice Perse of Kingsthorpe, was the bastard son of William Penifader.

In the center of Brigstock today, as in Cecilia Penifader's time, lies the church of St. Andrew. Some parts of the church are very old. The western tower and parts of the nave were built by Saxons, about a century before the Norman invasion of 1066. The church of St. Peter in Stanion is much the same—not quite as ancient, but also very old and centrally located in the original village. Yet many aspects of these buildings, as we can see them today, would have been unknown to Cecilia. Like so many English parish churches, St. Andrew and St. Peter were greatly improved by prosperous parishioners in the late fourteenth and fifteenth centuries, and the buildings we can visit today are as influenced by worship in our time as by medieval antecedents. Today, the churchyards of St. Andrew and St. Peter are sedate, quiet, and well-tended; Cecilia walked on church grounds filled with a hodgepodge of graves where people readily gathered for markets, ball games, gambling, gossip, sexual assignations, and perhaps even meetings of the manorial court. Hens, ducks, dogs, and other creatures also then made themselves comfortable around the graves of the human dead. Today, both churches are built of fine stone; Cecilia knew

St. Andrew's Church in Stanion as it appears today, seen from the left stands the bell tower, and below that is the porch through which people still enter and leave the nave. The chancel is on the right, located at the east end of the nave.

smaller churches with some parts built of wood and rubble as well as stone. Today, the interiors are filled with orderly pews, well-lit by electrical fixtures, and decorated with soft hues and whitened walls; Cecilia stood or squatted in pewless naves, relied on indirect natural light in the day or flickering candle-light at night, and looked up at colorful walls painted with scenes from Christian history and salvation.

Yet the biggest differences between then and now have less to do with the two church buildings in Brigstock parish and more to do with belief and ritual. Cecilia was a Christian, but she was a different sort of Christian from those found in Europe today. In part, these differences reflect changes in Christianity. In some regions of Europe, the Protestant reformers of the sixteenth century swept aside many of the beliefs of Cecilia's time, along with some of the oldest rituals of the medieval Church. They also introduced a diversity of Christian practice unknown to Cecilia. Although there were two main branches of Christianity in the Middle Ages—Catholicism centered in Rome and Orthodoxy centered in Constantinople (modern-day Istanbul)—Cecilia, living on the western periphery of Europe, knew only the teachings of the Catholic Church. Today, Roman Catholicism is the modern faith most closely tied to the teachings and practices of Christianity in Western Europe in the early fourteenth century, but it has changed considerably since the Middle Ages. Especially important in this regard have been the two reforming councils of Trent in 1545–62 and Vatican II in 1962–65.

In part, however, the differences between Cecilia's religiosity and modern Christian faiths also reflect changes rooted more in history than theology. First, Cecilia's religious world was strikingly homogeneous; she might have heard stories about Jews or heretics, but the world in which she lived offered no alternative religious practices. Jews had been expelled from England in 1290, a few years before Cecilia was born, and although the English heresy known as Lollardy developed a generation or so after she died, no heretics tempted country folk with radical interpretations of Christianity in early fourteenth-century England.[1] Sometimes Cecilia's neighbors worshipped at wells, cast spells, sought help from hermits, or established informal shrines. These folk practices were discouraged by the Church, but they usually accommodated easily to the predominant practices of medieval Christianity. Wells, spells, hermits, and shrines were readily associated with Christian holiness and Christian saints. Second, Cecilia's religious life was imbued by the rhythms of the natural world around her; she would not have thought it odd that she feared fairies as well as her Christian God, or that she mingled charms with prayers, or that major Christian holy days coincided with the summer and winter solstices. Third, her religious education was accomplished more by observation and listening than by study; Cecilia understood what it meant to be a Christian from what she *saw* in church (the ritual of the Mass, the wall paintings, the statues) and from what she *heard* in occasional sermons, pious songs and ballads, and the talk of her friends and family. Indeed, Cecilia's mother was probably her most important religious instructor. Joan of Arc, another peasant woman born in Lorraine in the early fifteenth century, testified that she learnt her prayers from her mother: "Nobody taught me my belief," she said, "if not my mother."

---

[1]Living in such a homogeneous world, Cecilia Penifader believed that many things were *facts* that are now considered to be *matters of faith*. For her, the basic tenets of medieval Christianity—such as the incarnation of Christ, the Resurrection, the sinless life of the Blessed Virgin Mary, and the miracles of the saints—were seen as undeniably real and true. To reflect her perspective, I have echoed her certainty in the text. So, for example, you will read about the feast of Pentecost as celebrating "when the Holy Ghost descended on the apostles," not "when, *according to Christian belief,* the Holy Ghost descended on the apostles."

PEASANT PIETY

Some historians have suggested that peasants like Cecilia were so poorly trained in Christianity and so devoted to traditional beliefs that they were not truly Christians. After all, when peasants wore animal masks at midwinter or danced around bonfires at midsummer, they echoed the customs of ancient pagans. Yet for Cecilia and others like her, there was no worship of older deities in these practices; instead, these were age-old customs that merged easily with Christianity. For the most part, folk traditions and Christianity were complementary not contradictory. Masking became part of Christmas revelries, and midsummer bonfires burned on the celebratory night before the feast of St. John the Baptist. The Church sometimes even encouraged these blendings of Christian practice and older custom. In the early seventh century, Gregory I had advised his missionaries to the Anglo-Saxons to convert pagan temples into Christian churches since people will be "more ready to come to the places with which they are familiar." Gregory was willing to make these concessions to ordinary folk because, as he put it, "it is impossible to cut out everything at once from their stubborn minds." Seven centuries later, peasants were still stubbornly fond of folk customs, and the clergy were still accommodating Christian beliefs to rural traditions.

For Cecilia and other medieval peasants, then, Church teachings, natural phenomena, and folk traditions merged easily into their understanding of religious belief and practice. In this blended form, Christianity permeated rural life. Cecilia may have prayed to the Blessed Virgin Mary as she mingled malt, yeast, and water to brew ale, or bowed her head when she passed a crucifix roughly built alongside a footpath, or whispered the Lord's Prayer before she entered the forest to gather herbs and nuts. These practices mingled superstition and piety, but they ensured that every day and in many ways, Cecilia sought the protection, help, and comfort of her God and his saints. As a young girl and a grown woman, Cecilia particularly focused her piety on the churches of St. Andrew and St. Peter. Two contemporary alternatives to parish-focused piety were not readily available to her because she was an illiterate peasant woman. First, private contemplation and pious reading were not very common, except among the wealthy. For example, before she died in 1360, the widowed Elizabeth de Burgh, Lady of Clare, enjoyed the daily support of her own private confessor and was also allowed to take a vow of chastity without entering a monastery. Many aristocrats even had their own private chapels in which they could worship, without having to resort to parish churches. No peasants had the leisure, education, or money for such pieties. At least one person in Brigstock owned a psalter (or book of psalms), but it was rare for a peasant to be able to read such a book or to be able to afford one (before the development of printing in the fifteenth century, books were handwritten and expensive). For Cecilia and her neighbors, formal religious efforts were mostly confined to church services on Sundays and holy days.

Second, a career in the Church was seldom available to peasants. Sometimes a peasant boy was accepted as a **deacon**, priest, friar, or monk, as

Cecilia's brother William seems to have been. But this was rare for boys, and it was nearly impossible for girls. Careers among the *secular clergy*, that is, among the clergy who ministered in the world to the souls of the faithful, were not available to women: there were no female deacons, priests, or bishops. Medieval people told a story about a Pope Joan, a woman who had begun to dress as a man to accompany her lover to university and who had then moved rapidly up the clerical hierarchy to become pope. Most such stories ended with Pope Joan dying in a papal procession, struck down by a difficult childbirth (or, in some versions, attacked by an angry mob after her birthing pains revealed her female identity). With its story of cross-dressing, illicit sex, and confused gender roles, the legend of Pope Joan titillated medieval listeners, but it had no basis in reality. From the pope in Rome to his bishops who oversaw **dioceses** throughout Europe to the priests who worked in parishes, the worldly work of the church was done by men.

A pious girl's main option for a professional religious life was among the *regular clergy* who lived by a monastic rule (or *regula*). To medieval Christians, monastic withdrawal was the ideal religious life. Unfortunately, most female monasteries required expensive dowries (or entry payments) from would-be nuns. This practice began in the early Middle Ages, and although popes and bishops tried hard to eradicate it, they were never successful; as a result, most female monasteries accepted only the daughters of wealthy parents who offered lucrative dowries. Moreover, even among wealthy women, monastic life was not readily available; the monasteries of England accommodated about three or four times as many monks as nuns. In England by 1300, there were about 6 million people but only 5,000 nuns.

Some female monasteries allowed poor women to work as *lay sisters*. Doing the chores that allowed nuns to focus on their prayers, lay sisters pursued holy lives, hoping to benefit spiritually from their hard work and their proximity to nuns. Lay sisters were helpers of nuns, not nuns themselves. For a few poor women and even fewer men, life in an **anchorhold** offered an alternative to monastic life. An anchorhold was a sort of hermitage, a small, enclosed space that was usually built alongside a church. The *anchoress* (or if male, *anchorite*) was permanently walled into this enclosure, observing holy services through a window that looked into the church, and receiving goods and visitors at a second outside window (or sometimes, door). Anchoresses and anchorites were more common in England than elsewhere, and they were tolerated by the Church but never fully integrated into the clergy. The most famous of medieval anchoresses, Juliana of Norwich, lived about 100 years after Cecilia in the East Anglian city from which she took her name. Her book *Revelations of Divine Love* still offers inspirational reading. Life in an anchorhold was hard, and chosen by only a few. All told, only a handful of peasant women ever managed to pursue pious lives as either lay sisters or anchoresses. For a woman like Cecilia, a life devoted to religion was not an option.

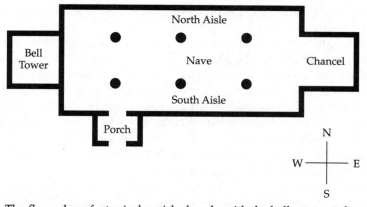

The floor plan of a typical parish church, with the bell tower to the west, the nave in the center, and the chancel to the east. The nave is divided by columns into a center and two aisles. Parishioners entered the church through the porch on the south side of the nave.

THE PARISH AND ITS CLERGY

The physical space of the churches of St. Andrew and St. Peter followed a pattern set long before the time of the Penifaders, a pattern used in almost all parish churches. They were long buildings, composed of two main rectangles: a small **chancel** (where the priest celebrated mass) in the east and a larger **nave** (where the parishioners gathered) in the west. The chancels of medieval churches and cathedrals were oriented to the east, that is, towards Jerusalem, the center of the medieval world.[2] Over time, the two rectangles of nave and chancel were slowly expanded; aisles were added to the nave to accommodate more parishioners, and eventually chapels were built alongside the chancel (at the east end of aisles) to accommodate the veneration of particular saints. The bell tower stood at the west end of the nave, and its bells regularly called people together, for holy services, to be sure, but also for deaths, fires, court meetings, and any other events that required everyone's attention. Along the south wall was always the door through which people entered and left. Outside, a porch protected this door from rain. At St. Peter's, more than fifty stone-carved heads of women, men, and animals ran, and still run today, above the porch and along the south wall. Cecilia would have looked at these carvings, completed just before her birth, whenever she went into St. Peter's or lingered in its churchyard. Masons often carved stone from standard patterns, but they sometimes chose models from local people. So it is possible that among the

[2]The dead were also buried facing Jerusalem, and for a similar reason, mapmakers placed east at the top (or sometimes center) of their maps. These practices suggest that medieval people saw their world on an east-west axis instead of a north-south axis.

faces along the south wall, Cecilia might have recognized her parents, her grandparents, and some of her neighbors.[3]

When Cecilia entered the church and stood in the nave, she watched the priest celebrating mass in the chancel directly in front of her, she heard the clatter of people entering and leaving to her right, and if she turned fully around, she faced the bell tower. During services, she stood or squatted with other women and girls, as the two sexes did not mingle together in church for fear, it seems, of sexual scandal in such a holy place. Around her the walls were painted with bright and vivid scenes that inspired wonder and fear. Today, no medieval paintings can be seen in the church of St. Andrew, and the two that survive in St. Peter's were completed about one hundred and fifty years after Cecilia's time. One shows a stag and a unicorn kneeling before a now-obscured figure, and the other depicts the Archangel Michael weighing souls to determine whether they should be saved or damned. The walls of other churches near Brigstock still contain holy scenes that suggest what Cecilia might have seen on the fourteenth-century walls of St. Peter's: The Last Judgment, the Virgin Mary, the Last Supper, the Crucifixion, St. Christopher, St. Catherine, and St. Margaret of Antioch.[4]

By custom, the chancel was the responsibility of the parish priest. If the roof leaked or the altar wobbled, he had to fix it. The nave and the rest of the church—that is, by far its largest part—was in the care of parishioners. If the door fell off its hinges or a bell cracked, then the parishioners of St. Andrew's had to raise the money to cover the work. Parishioners maintained what was called the *fabric* of the church through money-raising festivals (the most popular were church-ales, at which ale was sold for the benefit of the church), through collections, and sometimes through gifts from pious and community-minded parishioners. In April 1344, for example, Denise in the Lane gave a small piece of her land to St. Andrew's church, asking that income from it be used to pay for general maintenance. Yet as neither the parish priest nor his parishioners ever had much money to spare, sometimes the chancel roof did leak, the door did sway loosely, and the bell did ring untrue.

The appointment of a parish priest was a complicated business in the Middle Ages. To begin with, control of the appointment (that is, the **advowson**) did not always rest with the local bishop or other ecclesiastical authority. Instead, the person whose family had originally built the church often held its advowson. This had a certain logic to it. Some might protest that the Church should appoint its own parish priests, but lords and ladies could justifiably respond that *they* should choose the men who worked in churches that had been originally built by *their* ancestors and were still generously supported by *their* money. In the case of Brigstock, the king once held the advowson of Brigstock parish just as he held the manor, and he had once appointed a new parish priest whenever the old one died, retired, or resigned. In 1133, however,

[3]The drawings that open each chapter of this book are based on these carvings.
[4]Although popular in the Middle Ages, these three saints were among those removed from the Catholic calendar in 1969.

Henry I gave the parish in perpetuity to Cirencester Abbey (located about one hundred miles southwest of Brigstock).

Henry's gift is an example of another complication in the staffing of parishes. Ideally, a priest was appointed to care for a parish, but by his gift, Henry made Cirencester Abbey perpetually responsible for the souls of Brigstock. In effect, he made the Abbey the **rector** (or appointed parish priest) of Brigstock. By the late thirteenth century, some rectors were institutions (as Cirencester Abbey was for Brigstock), and many others were individuals; both sorts of rectors were often absentees who appointed other priests to do their work. For example, the monks of Cirencester could not travel regularly to Brigstock to care for its parishioners, so the Abbey appointed a priest to do the job. This priest was known as a **vicar,** because he acted in the place of the rector.[5] Some parishes were served directly by their rectors, but many others were under the care of a vicar, as Brigstock was. In most parishes with a vicar, the absentee rector took most of the income from the parish and paid the vicar a measly sum. In the case of Brigstock, William de Clive was vicar of Brigstock from 1275 to 1325, Roger de Corndale from 1325 to 1340, and John de Seymour from 1340 to 1344 (the year Cecilia died). Cirencester Abbey, as rector of Brigstock, took a hefty sum from the parish each year (more than £10), and then paid their vicar less than half of the takings (a bit over £4). As the history of the advowson, rectory, and vicarage of Brigstock parish shows so clearly, appointment to a parish had become by the fourteenth century a sort of commodity that could be owned by institutions as well as individual priests, and that could be bought, sold, or even traded. It was a source of income acquired by a lucky man or institution who often then hired someone else to do the work.

Supported by only a fraction of the parish income, the vicar of Brigstock nevertheless had to find money to pay others to help him in his work. Because Brigstock had two churches, the vicar had to hire a second priest to manage the church of St. Peter in Stanion. More than likely, these two priests were assisted by still others—perhaps a deacon or two and probably a **parish clerk.** Deacons were the chief assistants of parish priests; they helped at mass, read scriptures during services, and instructed parishioners. Parish clerks also assisted during holy services, but, as skilled secretaries, they especially busied themselves by reading and writing up the documents of the parish. The priests, deacons, and clerks who assisted the vicar of Brigstock are rarely mentioned in either manorial or ecclesiastical records, but it is likely that Cecilia's brother William was among them. William left Brigstock in 1308, and after he returned in 1317, he was always identified with the unusual and respectful title of *Magister* (or "Master"). Perhaps he held a degree from Oxford or Cambridge (as did many "Masters"), but more likely he was just much better educated than anyone else in Brigstock. He might have been the parish clerk or a

---

[5]Vicar literally meant substitute; it comes from the same Latin word from which we get such modern words as *vicarious* or *vice-president*. All the priests who worked in a parish, whether rectors, vicars, or their assistants, can be called **parsons,** a generic term used for all parochial priests.

deacon, but he was certainly well educated enough to be the second priest in Brigstock, appointed by the vicar to care for St. Peter's church in Stanion.

As one of a handful of churchmen in Brigstock parish, Master William personifies the ambivalent status of rural clergy. On the one hand, William was an ordinary person, a local boy. Older people remembered him as a child; his friends sweated beside him in field and pasture; children played with his nephews and nieces. Most days, he got up and did exactly what his neighbors did. He went into the fields to plow, sow, or weed; he tended to the health of his sheep; he cultivated fruits and vegetables in his garden. When he attended the manorial court every three weeks, he never served as a juror, **aletaster,** or other manorial officer, but he otherwise acted like his brothers. He purchased land from his neighbors, he pledged for the good conduct of his friends, and he proffered excuses for those unable to get to court.[6] Like everyone else in Brigstock, William was a peasant, well known to his neighbors and busied by the same tasks.

On the other hand, William, as a cleric, had special stature within Brigstock parish. First, he was better educated than most people. There were no seminaries to train priests in medieval Europe, so most would-be priests had to rely on local clergymen to teach them to read Latin and to train them in the rituals of the mass. William might have received some basic training from William de Clive, the vicar of Brigstock during his childhood, and for many priests, their education ended there. As a result, priests in rural parishes were often minimally trained for their duties. Some were so ignorant that they could barely mumble the first lines of the mass, and others even unwittingly led peasants into theological error. William's title of "Master" suggests that he received a better education than most priests, and when he left Brigstock for nine years, he may have studied with some learned men. His education was exceptional for a rural cleric. Yet whether highly educated or roughly trained, rural priests had more learning than their parishioners. Many read with difficulty and understood only rudimentary Latin, but they were, at least, literate.

Second, William was special because he did not marry, at least not in a technical sense. The Catholic Church had long encouraged priests to practice celibacy, and from the eleventh century, clerical marriage had been explicitly forbidden. Nevertheless, many priests interpreted this prohibition loosely. Some sought casual liaisons, and others, although they refrained from contracting legitimate marriages, settled down with women, fathered and raised children, and sometimes even trained sons to become clerics and take over the family business. Everyone looked the other way; it was irregular but it was common. William, for whom no "wife" is mentioned in the courts of Brigstock, had at least one child, the son John to whom he gave his properties in 1326. Alice Perse, the mother of this son, might have lived in Kingsthorpe, a village about eighteen miles southwest of Brigstock, or she might have moved

---

[6]Pledging was an important part of manorial courts. A **pledge** stood before the court to guarantee that another person would fulfill a stipulated obligation or pay a stipulated fine. Most transactions in manorial courts required the guarantee of a pledge, and almost all pledges were adult men.

from Kingsthorpe to live with William in Brigstock. If so, she lived like numerous other "priest's concubines" in medieval villages; much like other wives in most respects, they were always vulnerable to gossip, criticism, and even Church sanction. One medieval tale related how a priest's concubine reacted to word that the bishop was coming to inspect the parish and, among other things, order her to leave. Fixing up a basket of cakes, eggs, and other good foods, she set out to meet the bishop on the road. When he asked her where she was going and why, she replied, "I'm taking these gifts to your mistress who has lately been brought to childbed." The bishop, thus reminded of his own sexual relationship, left her and her family alone. William's family was also left alone. His son John not only inherited William's lands but also became a cleric like his father. Treated kindly by his aunt Cecilia when she was on her deathbed, John seems to have been an accepted and well-loved member of the Penifader family.

Third, William and other clerics enjoyed a special legal status. He was protected by the king's justice and he could be sued in civil courts for unpaid loans or other business gone wrong, but if he committed a crime, he was punished in ecclesiastical courts, not secular ones. "Criminous clerks" had been the cause of a great argument at the end of the twelfth century, an argument that had pitted Thomas Becket, then Archbishop of Canterbury, against his former friend and king, Henry II. Becket supported the Church's claim to judge clerics under the procedures of canon law; Henry II thought it outrageous that he could not punish all those who committed offenses within his realm. Becket lost his life in this argument, killed before the altar of Canterbury by four knights who thought they were carrying out the wishes of Henry II. But Becket's viewpoint finally prevailed. Arrangements differed throughout medieval Europe, but in most places, the Church successfully asserted its right to judge clerics for rape, murder, arson, treason, theft, fraud, and other offenses.

Fourth, if, as is likely, William was ordained as a priest, he was also a special person in Brigstock because of his sacerdotal powers. Of all the people in Brigstock, only he and the vicar could celebrate the mass, impose penance on sinners, anoint the dying, and otherwise ensure, through their special powers, God's grace and God's salvation. As someone empowered to administer the sacraments of the Church, he stood as a critical intermediary between ordinary people and their God. A priest's words were understood to transform bread and wine into the body and blood of Christ; his absolution wiped away sins; his blessings baptized infants, sanctified marriages, and eased the dead toward salvation. If the Penifaders saw William celebrating mass when they went to St. Peter's on Sunday, they understood little of the Latin he muttered and not much about the symbolic significance of all he did, but they knew that he, alone of all of them, had a special relationship to the bread and wine, the body and blood of Christ.

The duties of the vicar of Brigstock and his assistants were carefully specified. They were to celebrate mass every day; they were to preach sermons at least four times each year; they were to teach their parishioners about the

A tutor with his pupils. Formal education was usually available only to boys destined for careers in the Church, and even these boys sometimes received minimal training. Most peasants never learned to read.

fourteen points of the creed, the Ten Commandments, the seven sacraments, and the seven deadly sins; they were to be sure that everyone confessed their sins and took communion at least once a year; they were to baptize the young, marry the nubile, and bury the dead. Whether priests did all this or not was mostly left up to their own consciences. Although bishops visited rural districts to search for incompetent or lazy priests, their visits were neither frequent nor effective. The Bishop of Lincoln and his subordinates sometimes asked the vicar of Brigstock to report his doings to them, but they seldom verified his responses by directly visiting the parish. The care of the souls of Brigstock was left almost wholly to the discretion of its vicar and his helpers. Perhaps many children learned their catechism, as did Joan of Arc, more from their mothers than from their parsons.

The clergy of Brigstock took their "living" from the parish in several ways. The vicar himself managed the *glebe*, lands in the parish assigned to his use. Like the demesne and the holdings of peasants, the glebe was usually scattered through the fields of a manor. Some priests leased out the glebe to others, but most worked it, like any other peasant, with their own muscle and sweat. In addition to the glebe, Cirencester Abbey assigned 22 shillings of rent to the vicar of Brigstock. In other words, there were a few tenants in the parish whose houses were owned by the Abbey and whose rent supported the vicar. Aside from the glebe and any rents that might accrue to the parish, most of a priest's living came directly from parishioners. Everyone paid **oblations,** that is, they paid (in cash or kind) for the services rendered by the priest. When the Penifader children were baptized, Robert and Alice paid for the priest's labor; when their children Emma and Alice died, they paid for their burials; when Christina and Agnes were married, they paid the priest to officiate; and when they confessed their sins and took communion, they paid for his assistance. In theory, these payments were voluntary, but in practice they were expected and required. Everyone in the parish was also required to tithe by contributing one-tenth of their yearly gains to the parish—every tenth sheaf at harvest, every tenth lamb born each spring, every tenth bucket of nuts from the forest, every tenth egg, every tenth of every sort of produce. Some Christians today tithe voluntarily, but in the Middle Ages it was compulsory, and it was also resented. In addition, in Brigstock and many other parishes, a *mortuary* was customarily due on the death of every head of a household. Based on the assumption that a dead person left behind unpaid tithes, the **mortuary** gave to the rector the second best animal of the deceased. More than likely, profits from tithes and mortuaries went directly to Cirencester Abbey, for their agreement with the vicar stipulated that he would keep only his glebe, his 22 shillings of rent, and his profits from oblations.

The vicar's assistants patched together their livings as best they could. Usually the vicar paid each assistant a small sum from his own income, and assistants also took oblations from parishioners. Master William, of course, had his own lands and house, so in addition to the money he got from the vicar and parishioners, he lived off properties he inherited or purchased. Other clerics made do as best they could. Absolon, the fictional cleric in the *Canterbury Tales,* made extra money by writing charters and other documents for his neighbors, but he also practiced medicine, barbered, and perhaps earned some money by singing and playing his guitar.

The churches of St. Andrew and St. Peter were familiar and comfortable places for Cecilia. She visited them often, she contributed to their upkeep, and she knew one of their clerics very well indeed. For her, as for most medieval peasants, parish churches were much more than sacred places visited on Sundays and other holy days. As the most substantial building in a village, the parish church was readily used for many purposes that some might label profane. People sometimes stored grain, cloth, or animals in the parish church, and they gathered in it to debate local issues as well as to worship their God. After all, the building was strong, and it was maintained by local funds. As long as its use as a storehouse, meeting place, or even indoor market was confined to the nave (away from the sacred space of the chancel), no harm was done.

As a familiar gathering spot, the parish church sometimes inspired more chatter than prayer. A perennial complaint of parsons was that their parishioners did everything during mass *except* pay attention to the sacred business at hand. Priests even gave sermons about a special demon, Tutivillus, who took notes on women's chatter in church; since he had so much gossip to write down, Tutivillus had to stretch his parchment by grasping it with teeth and feet, and in so doing, he lost his balance and cracked his head. The lesson was a funny one, intended to teach that talk in church, particularly the talk of women, was the devil's delight. This was a much-ignored lesson. Most parishioners attended church regularly, but they did not necessarily feel compelled to pay close attention to what the priest and his assistants did at the altar. Perhaps, they were satisfied to have made it to church at all, instead of lingering in bed or stopping at an alehouse. So, while the mass was celebrated by Master William in the chancel of St. Peter's, some parishioners in the nave recited prayers and pondered the miracle of the Eucharist, but others discussed spring plowing, gossiped about a stranger met on the road, or planned a trip for the next Friday to the weekly market in Kettering. In short, like the men who served as its priests, deacons, and clerks, the parish church negotiated between sacred and everyday functions. It was holy space, but it was also community space.

THE RITUAL YEAR

This same mingling of sacred and profane was true of the calendar that structured the lives of Cecilia and her family. For the Penifaders, the year had no clear beginning or end. The modern designation of January 1st as New Year's Day was as old as Rome itself, but in the early fourteenth century, it was eclipsed as a holiday by Christmas a week earlier and the feast of Epiphany a few days later. (Epiphany commemorated the arrival of the Magi, or Wise Men, to visit the infant Jesus and his mother in the manger.) For the clerks who kept calendars, the year officially changed on March 25th, the feast celebrating the Annunciation of the Blessed Virgin Mary (that is, the appearance of the archangel Gabriel before Mary to announce that she was pregnant). The Annunciation was neatly timed exactly nine months before the birth of Jesus in the Christian calendar. For Cecilia, however, "Ladyday" probably passed without much notice in the midst of Lent and spring planting. A third annual shift coincided with the end of harvest, and was linked to Michaelmas, the feast of St. Michael on September 29. Clerks and accountants usually figured years from one September 29th to the next, counting acres, seed, and bushels; paying workers and creditors; and adding up their figures in preparation for audit. Live-in servants were hired either at Michaelmas or a few weeks later, agreeing to serve year-long contracts.

Yet if Cecilia's year had no clear beginning or end, it was punctuated by many holidays. She worked hard, but she also often rested and often played. The calendar of the Church dictated a great deal of this schedule of work and leisure (which explains why our word "holiday" derives from "holy day"). By Cecilia's time, holy days and Sundays accounted for about one hundred days a year—or about one of every four days. On Sundays, work in the fields was discouraged, and while women might have mended clothes and men sharpened tools, it was mostly a day of rest. An additional forty-odd days, concentrated around Christmas and Easter but otherwise scattered throughout the year, were special holy days on which no one did much work. The Church's designation of holy days ran along two primary axes. The first set commemorated the story of Jesus' life and work as understood by Christians through the New Testament, and the second celebrated notable events in the lives of various saints. In Brigstock parish, the feasts of the patron saints of the two churches—St. Peter (June 29th) and St. Andrew (November 30th)—would have been especially observed, and for Cecilia, the feast of St. Cecilia (November 22nd) would have been a special day, probably more important than her birthday. With all of Christendom, Cecilia and the parishioners of Brigstock also rested for two long periods each year—for the Twelve Days between Christmas and Epiphany, and for all of Easter Week.

Christmas was a time of special festivity. Like everyone else, Cecilia fasted through December, restricting her diet, perhaps no meats or tasty sauces, for the four weeks of Advent that preceded Christmas. On Christmas morning, her piety was rewarded. As people gathered in church in the cold darkness before dawn, they were met with an abundance of candles and a celebratory service. Afterwards, the feasting would begin, and some people were so eager to start the fun that they skipped the holy services. One grim but popular medieval story tells of twelve people who sang and danced in front of their church at Christmas; when the priest called them to services and they refused to come, he cursed them; for an entire year thereafter, they were condemned to dance in an endlessly wearying frenzy; when the curse was finally lifted at the next Christmas, some died, and the rest were condemned to wander the countryside, afflicted with agitated minds and twitchy limbs. A tale like this probably did a great deal to encourage Cecilia and her family to attend Christmas services and to wait patiently for the feasting and dancing that was to come.

By tradition, the wealthy opened their houses at Christmas, feeding the humble and poor. On manors with resident lords or ladies, free tenants and serfs could expect just this sort of beneficence, that is, a feast of fine meats and strong ale in the hall of the manor house. In Brigstock, perhaps the Penifaders and other well-off peasants fed their poorer neighbors, or perhaps the parishioners pooled their resources for a common feast. However it was staged, the Christmas feast signaled the beginning of twelve festive days when people put aside work to eat, dance, tell stories, wear masks and costumes, and play. In grand houses, professional entertainers—harpers, minstrels, and actors—provided amusement; in Brigstock, the songs, dances, and stories must have come from local talent.[7] For Cecilia and her family, the twelve days of Christmas brought no feasts in manor houses and no professional entertainment, but they were days of full stomachs and tipsy heads. It was a good way to get through some of the darkest and coldest days of the year when neither fields nor flocks demanded much work. The worst of winter would soon be past.

On January 6th, the Twelve Days ended with a dramatic Epiphany service commemorating the arrival of the Magi and one final feast. Then, it was back to work, and especially to plowing the fields in anticipation of spring planting. In Brigstock, as in many villages, the transition to work was probably a gentle one; on the Monday after Epiphany, men secured blessings for their plows in the parish church and then dragged them through streets and lanes, cajoling money out of everyone they encountered. The money raised on "Plow Mon-

---

[7]In many places, the festivities also included an element of controlled disorder and misrule. For a few hours, a servant might be crowned king, a novice monk made abbot, or an apprentice elevated to mayor. This "feast of fools," as it was sometimes called, ultimately served more to reinforce hierarchy than to ridicule it. It was popular in aristocratic courts, monasteries, and towns, but it seems never to have been adopted by the English peasantry.

day" was then put to charitable uses—perhaps to fix a loose door or recast a bell, or perhaps to aid parish orphans and other unfortunates.

A few weeks later, work paused briefly for one of the most beautiful services in the Christian calendar: the commemoration of the Purification of the Virgin on February 2nd. The Old Testament had required that new mothers be purified in a ritual bath several weeks after giving birth; medieval Christians adapted this Jewish tradition not only in their commemoration of the Virgin Mary but also in **churching** ceremonies for new mothers. Each new mother in Brigstock went to church about six weeks after childbirth to celebrate her successful delivery. The medieval service stressed thanksgiving rather than purification, but its purifying implications persisted. In some parishes, women who died in childbirth (that is, without the benefit of churching) were refused burial in holy ground. Cecilia's mother Alice celebrated eight churchings over some twenty years, each time thanking God for her safe delivery and enjoying the congratulations of the women—kin and friends—who had assisted in her perilous labor. These churchings could be so happy and festive that in some towns, authorities had to step in to control crowds and to limit the "dishes, meats, and wines" consumed afterwards. In Brigstock, we know of no churchings that caused too much public commotion, but they were surely joyous occasions, with the new mother thanking God for her delivery, her friends and family offering their congratulations, and everyone celebrating the mother's successful passage through the perils of childbirth.

The feast of the Purification of the Virgin, then, was especially important to the mothers of Brigstock. As they gathered with everyone else on the second day of February, Alice and the other mothers of Brigstock may have felt a particular kinship with the Virgin who, like them, had offered thanks for a successful labor. The feast of the Purification also marked, as Groundhog Day now does in the United States, the early turning of winter into spring, and it was celebrated, appropriately enough, with dramatic darkness and dramatic

Parishioners carrying candles on the Feast of the Purification of the Virgin Mary (also known as Candlemas). The candles blessed at this service were thought to ward off evil, illness, and other troubles.

light. Lit with an extraordinary display of candles, the church of St. Andrew welcomed the Penifaders out of the cold dawn of a February morning. After the mass, everyone paraded around the church with candles, and when this procession ended, other candles and tapers were blessed and then saved for later use (they were considered to be especially useful for warding off demons or other evils). The candles were so bright in the darkness of early morning that the service was familiarly known as Candlemas. Afterwards feasting began, and having fasted the day before, everyone ate with enthusiasm.

Within a few weeks, parishioners began to prepare for the Easter season. As the major movable feast in the Christian calendar, Easter fell on the first Sunday after the first full moon after the vernal equinox—a date that could fall anywhere between March 22nd and April 25th. Each year, the forty days before Easter were times of particular fasting and self-denial (even more so than the four weeks of Advent). Before Lent began, everyone enjoyed one last party: Shrovetide. The winter stocks of foods that would be forbidden during Lent—meat, eggs, cheese, and so on—were eaten, and then, on Ash Wednesday, the fast began. The next forty days were a somber time. Everyone ate a restricted diet; no festivities eased work; and religious sculptures, paintings, or other images in the churches of St. Andrew and St. Peter were veiled from human view. These were also critical weeks in the agricultural year. Fields were plowed, sown, and harrowed; ewes were brought through lambing; and houses were swept out and spruced up in spring cleaning. With half-empty stomachs and a shrouded church, Cecilia and her family might have thought much about sin and redemption during Lent, but they also worked hard. Fortunately, they must have also relished the warming weather, increasing daylight, new flowers, migrating birds, and newborn lambs of spring.

The final week of Lent was Holy Week. On the last Sunday before Easter, the Penifaders brought branches to be blessed, a celebration of spring growth that also remembered the palms strewn before Jesus as he entered Jerusalem. Especially grave services followed all week, and then, on Friday, the crucifixion was commemorated. Later generations of English peasants built Easter sepulchers for this part of Holy Week—miniature tombs surrounded by candles and watched by the faithful between Friday and Sunday—but it is not known whether people in Cecilia's time had already developed this custom. Nevertheless, they surely gathered in church on Saturday night, extinguished all candles and flames, and then lit them anew, brightening the church with the largest candle of the ritual year, the paschal candle. Early Sunday morning, after forty days of moderate fast and a week of intensifying observances, the Penifaders celebrated the Resurrection in a church joyously returned to its old state—candles lit, statues unveiled, and paintings revealed. They brought with them eggs to be blessed, for even in the early fourteenth century, eggs were already a dual symbol of Easter and spring. After the Easter mass, everyone in Brigstock enjoyed several days of feasts and games. The celebrations were not as long or as intense as those of the Twelve Days of Christmas, but they were more likely to be outside. The Penifaders watched, participated in,

A dancing woman.

and enjoyed archery contests, ball games, wrestling, tumbling, dancing, and singing in the aftermath of Holy Week.

   After Easter, a variety of lesser holidays relieved the work of late spring and early summer. On May Day, Cecilia and her sisters probably rose before dawn and gathered flowers to decorate themselves and their house. Later, they danced with local boys around the maypole, a custom that possibly dated from Anglo-Saxon times. May Day was a holiday of particular importance to the young, but everyone joined in the predawn walks, the selection of the maypole, the dancing, and the feasting. Ascension was the next important holiday, following Easter by six weeks and celebrating the bodily ascent of the resurrected Christ into heaven. On the Monday, Tuesday, and Wednesday before Ascension (known as Rogation Days), Cecilia and her sisters might have watched as their father and brothers walked the boundaries of the parish, a practice designed to ensure that each generation remembered the trees, ditches, and hedges that marked off the jurisdiction of Brigstock. In many parishes, boys were beaten at critical junctures, to ensure that boundary markers were forever impressed on their minds. Perhaps Cecilia's brothers Henry, Robert, and William endured, as boys, this cruel but effective custom known as *beating the bounds*. Less than two weeks later, everyone commemorated

Whitsun, a feast celebrating Pentecost, when the Holy Ghost descended on the apostles. Whitsun usually fell during the fine weather of June, and it was often observed with parades, dances, games, and feasting. Many parishes took advantage of the good weather to hold church-ales, using the festivities to raise money for parochial projects. Throughout May and June, the Penifaders and their neighbors continued to work hard—plowing fallow fields, weeding sown acres, fixing drainage ditches, checking flocks, and making hay.

Then, as haymaking ended at midsummer, work stopped for the bonfires of St. John's Eve, the night before the feast that commemorated the birth of St. John the Baptist on June 24th. We celebrate the solstice on June 21st; medieval people considered that midsummer coincided with St. John's Eve, a small shift that neatly accommodated nature to the religious calendar. On St. John's Eve, the people of Brigstock gathered on a nearby hill, built huge piles of twigs, wood, and straw; and then, when the sun finally set on the longest day of the year, chased away the dark with fire. As she stood sweating from the blaze and panting from the dancing, Cecilia may have felt protected by the fire. Medieval children were taught that the fires of St. John's Eve guarded them from summer infections and saved the ripening crops from blight.

The time between midsummer and Advent was perhaps the busiest time in Brigstock. In late June and July, fields needed to be weeded and plowed; in August and September, harvest ruled the day; and in October and November, the Penifaders were busy slaughtering pigs, collecting fruits and nuts, and otherwise preparing for winter. In these months, only three dates loomed large. On June 29th, the church of St. Peter in Stanion celebrated the feast day of its saint, and the church of St. Andrew in Brigstock did the same on November 30th. Some churches mounted large church-ales on such days and used the occasion to collect money for church repairs or charitable uses, but in Brigstock parish, neither saint's day fell at a convenient time. The celebration of the feast of St. Peter might have often been eclipsed by the still smoldering fires of St. John's Eve, and the combination of cold weather and Advent probably ensured a modest feast in commemoration of St. Andrew. Aside from these two special days in the parish of Brigstock, only one holy day was particularly important to Christians in these months: on November 1st, the feast of All Saints marked the beginning of winter. At the moment that nature itself seemed to be dying or preparing for death, Cecilia and others remembered the human dead. In the dark afternoon, with dead leaves underfoot, and an uncertain supply of food put aside for winter, they began to ring the bells of St. Andrew and St. Peter—to comfort the dead, as they had been taught—and they continued their somber task well into the night. Less than a month later, Advent began.

Today, many things can seem familiar about the ritual year that set the pace of Cecilia's life. We can link Plow Monday with the ritual of blessing tractors in some parts of modern Germany; the Purification of the Virgin with the custom of Groundhog Day in the United States; the feasting of Shrovetide with Pancake Day in Britain as well as Mardi Gras in New Orleans; the branches blessed before Easter with modern Palm Sunday; the fires of

St. John's Eve with midsummer bonfires still seen in northern Europe; the sad remembrances of All Saints with Halloween; even the rhythms of planting and harvesting with today's academic calendar (which offers its longest breaks during the heaviest seasons of agricultural work).

Yet Cecilia's year was different from our own. For us, May Day, midsummer, and Halloween are pleasant interruptions in modern schedules far removed from the dictates of nature. For Cecilia, the natural cycles of the year—light and dark, warm and cold, work and leisure—were strongly echoed in the ritual calendar. For many of us, religious rituals are comforting but somewhat distant from our everyday lives. For Cecilia, they often spoke not only about holy events and holy persons but also about her own life and her own experiences: about the churching of her mother on the feast of the Purification of the Virgin; about the coming work of harvest on St. John's Eve; about the deaths of her sisters Emma and Alice on All Saints. For most of us, food and fire are controllable things, available when we need them and easily put aside when we do not. Yet Cecilia would have thought it foolish to count so confidently on food and light. She saw people sicken and die from inadequate diets, and she accommodated her work to the light of the sun and the dark of a night lit only by the moon. For her, these rituals—which so often asked her to fast and then feast, to feel darkness and then see light—spoke powerfully about things that she could not fully control. So in real and direct ways, the ritual year of Brigstock spoke about the life of Cecilia, about her religious faith, to be sure, but also about her natural world, her experiences, and her fears.

SUGGESTIONS FOR FURTHER READING

Although it focuses on a later period, Ronald Hutton's *The Rise and Fall of Merry England: The Ritual Year, 1400–1700* (1994) is an excellent introduction to many rural practices, beliefs, and rituals. See also Eamon Duffy, *The Stripping of the Altars: Traditional Religion in England 1400–1580* (1992); Ronald C. Finucane, *Miracles and Pilgrims: Popular Beliefs in Medieval England* (1995); and the old but still useful study of sermon literature by G. R. Owst, *Literature and Pulpit in Medieval England* (1961). For ecclesiastical history and religious practice, see two books by R. N. Swanson, *Church and Society in Late Medieval England* (1989) and *Religion and Devotion in Europe, c. 1215–c. 1515* (1995).

CHAPTER 5

Changing Times

In September 1319, John Tulke sold two small properties in the court of Brigstock. The first went to Robert, son of Henry Kroyl, and the second went to Cecilia Penifader. Cecilia promised to pay the court 6 pence to allow this transfer, and her brother-in-law Henry Kroyl stood as her pledge for the transaction.

When Cecilia Penifader was approaching adulthood, her world was shattered by famine. Late in 1314, unusually heavy rains began to fall, and they fell for months on end, drenching the fields even in spring and summer. The harvest that August was disappointing, and thereafter, weather and harvests got even worse. The winter of 1315 was exceptionally cold, and for several years, bad weather was more common than not. Too much cold and too much rain blighted the land. For the people who lived in southern Europe, this temporary spate of wet and cold weather was not a problem and might even have been a relief. But for the people of northern Europe, such weather was disastrous. Wet weather meant bad harvests. Bad harvests meant less food. Less food meant hunger and possibly starvation. The years from 1315 to 1322 were bad years.

The court rolls of Brigstock tell about sales of land, straying animals, and petty crimes; they do not report directly about bad harvests, diseased animals, or Penifaders weakened by hunger. Yet there are many *indirect* suggestions that people in Brigstock struggled especially hard in these years. Many more of them than ever before were accused of stealing sheaves, pilfering hay, or **gleaning** without permission (gleaners gathered up small bits of grain left on an already harvested field). Many more people than before took on debts they could not repay. Many more, like John Tulke in the case that opens this chapter, tried to make ends meet by selling small bits of land to their better-off neighbors. All of these things suggest that many people in Brigstock were adding desperate measures, including theft, debt, and land-sales, to their economy of makeshifts.

Cecilia lost her parents in these years. Robert was dead by 1318 (when Cecilia's brother Robert went to court as his father's executor); Alice never appeared in court after 1319, so she probably soon followed her husband to the grave. It is unlikely that Robert and Alice starved to death. As relatively well-off villagers, they suffered less than many of their poorer neighbors in Brigstock. But as old people, they were especially weakened by the hardships that began in 1315. In this famine, as is still the case today, young children and the elderly were at high risk, and they died less often from starvation than from diseases and accidents that befell their weakened bodies. The court rolls cannot tell us how many young nieces and nephews Cecilia might have lost in the Great Famine, but by the time it was over, her parents were gone.

THE GREAT FAMINE, 1315–22

The Great Famine is justly named. It was the worst famine Europe had ever seen or has seen since. Bad weather was the precipitating cause, but the weather was fortuitous, not part of a long-term trend. Despite the cold and wet weather of the famine years, the European climate gradually warmed between 1100 and 1350. Chroniclers complained in 1314 and after about unusually heavy rains and cold winters. They wrote about heavy downpours, frightening storms, flooded fields, and frigid air. Botanists today have confirmed what the chroniclers then observed. By checking the growth rings of ancient oaks (trees that grow quickly in rainy years), they have found exceptional development between 1315 and 1318. As the rains fell and the oaks grew, fields flooded, seed washed away, grain rotted, and flocks suffered. One Englishman wrote about these years, "Came never a disaster into England that made men more aghast."

The weather improved slightly after 1318, but it was unsteady well into the 1320s. More importantly, the damage done in 1315–18 had a rippling effect on arable and animal husbandry that lasted well beyond the hardest years of heavy rains and bitter cold. On the arable land of Brigstock, the rains took a heavy toll. They made it difficult to maneuver plows through wet, heavy soil; they damaged the productivity of the soil by leeching nitrates from it; they washed away seed; they provided an ideal environment for mildew, mold, and other crop diseases; they beat down the growing stalks before they could be harvested. Even before 1315, the Penifaders and their neighbors had labored in the fields for returns that were pathetically low by modern standards; they took about 4 bushels of grain for every bushel sown. From this, they would eat 3 bushels and set the fourth aside for next year's seed. The rains

Harvest scene. Peasants are stacking sheaves of grain into a cart.
During the Great Famine, harvest carts were—like the one pictured
here—more empty than full.

that began in 1314 lowered the 1:4 yield ratio to dangerous levels: sometimes
3, sometimes 2, sometimes less than 1 bushel harvested for every bushel sown.
These yields presented the peasants of northern Europe with a devil's bargain,
a choice between hunger now or hunger later. If the Penifaders harvested
2 bushels of wheat from a plot that usually yielded 4 bushels, they faced immediate hunger, but they also faced long-term hunger if they ate both bushels
(for they needed to save one bushel for seed). This was a hard choice, and it
worked to extend the famine beyond the years of the most difficult weather.
As the quality and quantity of seed declined, so too did the harvest.

The animals on whom the Penifaders depended so much for draft power,
food, and fertilizer also suffered horribly in the famine. Animals felt the cold
as much as humans, freezing in pastures and fields. They felt hunger too, for
the pastures were not as rich as before and fodder was hard to come by. Animals also died of *murrains*, epidemic diseases that began to spread rapidly
among oxen, cattle, and sheep. These diseases left their victims so disgustingly
dead, their carcasses putrefying rapidly and smelling horribly, that no meat or
hides could be salvaged from them. If the Penifaders were like most peasants,
they lost about half of their herd and flock, if not more. These losses were not
easily replaced, especially with the weakened stock that remained. It took
years—in some cases 20 years—to build herds and flocks back to their pre-
1315 strength.

Both parts of the mixed farming regime of Brigstock, then, were hit hard
by the famine. The fields yielded less stubble and fodder for animal consumption, and as animals died, there were fewer oxen or horses to pull the plows
and less manure to enrich the soil. This was a dangerous downward spiral.
Yet the peasants of Brigstock survived these hard years better than most.
Compared to townspeople, peasants were somewhat insulated from the worst
effects of the famine since they could more readily search for extra food in
woodland and field. Townspeople produced some of their own food (many
kept pigs or chickens and tended small gardens), but they had to buy most of

what they ate. When they went to the market during the Great Famine, they found food to be highly priced and in short supply. In the autumn of 1315, the price of wheat rose by almost 50 percent in just a few weeks; by the next summer, townspeople were buying wheat, if they could find it, at almost five times its prefamine price. Those who could not pay these outrageous prices either starved within town walls or began to wander the countryside in search of food.

Peasants could forage for food in many ways, and the peasants of Brigstock, with the resources of Rockingham Forest around them, had better foraging than most. They poached deer and hare in the royal preserve; they found plants or barks that were disagreeable, but edible; they perhaps even tried eating grubs, rats, and other vermin. When crops failed and animals died, these peculiar diets eased considerably the grumbling stomachs of the Penifaders and their neighbors, offering some nourishment as well as some comfort.[1] Our best estimates suggest that about 10 percent of the population died during the famine, but more died in town than in the country, and many died not of starvation but of diseases that opportunistically attacked their weakened bodies (typhoid seems to have been the main culprit). The young and old were especially vulnerable, as were those who were already poor. It is possible that men, less protected by body fat, suffered more than women.[2]

Brigstock saw many more changes than just peculiar diets during these years. Neighborliness broke down. Faced with bad harvests, people turned more than before to petty crime in the open fields; they contracted more debts they could not repay; they sold off more and more land. The incidence of these problems doubled during the famine, and in every case they created grievances—including missing grain, money not repaid, and lands unwillingly sold—between neighbors. After all, once Richard Everard suspected that Cecilia and her father had pilfered hay from him in the summer of 1316 (his complaint was described at the opening of chapter 2), he must have watched his Penifader neighbors with a new sharpness and resentment. Neighborliness was also aggravated by lack of charity and hoarding, for the hungry deeply resented neighbors who had food they would not share or sell. In ordinary times, the poor of Brigstock were supported by charity from kin or neighbors, by the support of parish and clergy, and sometimes even by parties thrown for their benefit (at a *help-ale*, for example, everyone paid high prices for ale, so that the poor host or hostess would benefit from the profits). During the Great Famine, these charitable activities temporarily declined, and prosperous families, like the Penifaders, hoarded what little they

---

[1]Chroniclers wrote about desperate people digging up corpses to eat or otherwise engaging in acts of cannibalism, but it is unlikely that famine diets were as peculiar as this. More than likely, chroniclers used this image, probably well known to them from earlier histories, to emphasize as best they could the horrible hunger of the people around them.

[2]Of course, this supposition assumes that food was distributed without regard to age or sex. It is possible, for example, that some women stinted themselves during the famine to better feed their children and husbands, and if so, the biological advantage of their extra body fat would have been offset by disadvantageous social practices.

had. Neighborly goodwill was undermined still further by the brisk market in land, as it is clear that some peasants used the misfortunes of their fellow villagers to accumulate larger holdings. Cecilia did just that. In 1319, when John Tulke was so desperate for money that he sold off some of his lands, Cecilia was ready to buy. She did the same on five other occasions during these years, so that by the time the famine ended, she controlled properties once held by John Tulke, Richard Koyk, and Ralph de la Breche. Their misfortune was her opportunity.

At the same time as the people of Brigstock were foraging with new inventiveness for food and watching their neighbors with more suspicion than before, they also had to contend with many impoverished strangers. Beggars and vagabonds had always wandered through Brigstock in search of charity and work, but their numbers swelled during the famine. Through the lanes of Brigstock came a steady stream of laborers looking for work—smallholders who had been forced to sell their lands and take to the road, servants let go by their employers, refugees searching for any food whatsoever, and beggars who could no longer rely on charity from nearby monasteries. They came singly, in gangs, and with families. To Cecilia, it must have seemed as if strangers arrived in Brigstock every day, hungry strangers who seemed pathetic and dangerous. Some might have died on the roads around Brigstock, others might have garnered a bit of work or bread from the Penifaders, and still others were doubtless chased away lest they take some food or goods not rightfully theirs.

THE WRATH OF GOD?

Between 1315 and 1322, the people of Brigstock looked with horror at rain-soaked fields, sickened cattle, unpleasant new foods, grasping neighbors, and frightening tramps. They filled the grounds around the churches of St. Andrew and St. Peter with the bodies of the young, the old, and the poor. They also prayed with new vigor, for it seemed clear that these disasters must be the work of a God who, as one contemporary put it, had sent "dearth on earth." In the summer of 1315, as the rains were ruining the first harvest of the Great Famine, the Archbishop of Canterbury ordered the clergy to respond immediately. They were to organize solemn processions of barefooted penitents accompanied by bells, relics, and prayers; they were to celebrate special masses; and they were to urge their people to fast, pray, and give alms. By these measures, the Archbishop hoped to appease the anger of God and to halt the terrible rains.

With the hindsight of many centuries, historians now explain the Great Famine in different ways. The bad weather that so ruined the fields and flocks of Brigstock remains inexplicable, but it is clear that bad weather was aggravated by other serious problems. First, the countryside was sorely overpopulated, a result of more than two centuries of extraordinary demographic growth. There were about 6 million people in England in 1300—about three times as many people as at the Norman Conquest of 1066, and many more

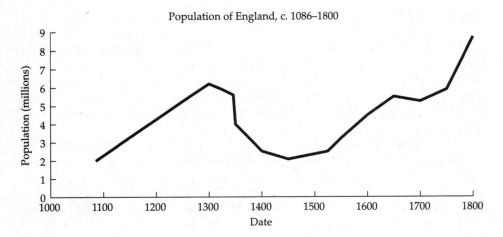

Population of England, c. 1086–1800

people than England would again support until after 1750. More than 900 adults and probably as many children lived in Brigstock and Stanion in 1300; that is, almost the same number of people who live in these two villages today. Even without famine, feeding these mouths was a problem. Second, the land was yielding less food. To feed their families, peasants took in more assarts, turning wasteland into arable and pasture. Eventually, they began to colonize moors, heaths, and other lands that were not very fertile. It is startling but true that in the early fourteenth century peasants tilled lands that modern farmers, armed with chemical fertilizers and heavy machinery, now avoid. In Cecilia's time, peasants worked more land, but took less from it. The conjunction of these two problems, rising population and inadequate productivity, created what historians today call a *Malthusian crisis:* too little food for too many mouths.[3]

By 1300, this crisis was adding more misery to the already difficult lives of medieval peasants. When Cecilia's older brother Henry began to seek paid work in Brigstock about 1300, he got low wages—because there were many hands eager for work at such rates. When he looked to rent some land, he had to pay higher rents—because lands were so scarce. When he purchased food, he had to pay high prices that seemed to be getting worse every year—because demand for foodstuffs was high. When he tried to bring wasteland into cultivation, he sweated over marginal lands that yielded disappointing returns— because all the good land was already taken. At every turn, he found bad options and frustration. The result of the discouraging circumstances faced by Henry Penifader and others was swift and predictable: population began to

---

[3]In 1798, Thomas Malthus argued in *An Essay on Population* that populations tend to grow faster than productive resources. Malthus used this trend to suggest that the poor, because they failed to restrict births, were responsible for their own poverty. This conclusion was controversial in Malthus' day and remains controversial today. Nevertheless, historians now use his ideas about the changing balance between people and resources to study past societies.

level off and then decline. For historians, it is unclear whether this demographic adjustment was caused by rising mortality or falling fertility. Perhaps poorer diets hastened some people into early graves, or perhaps anxiety about hungry mouths prompted some couples, such as Henry and his wife who together produced only three grown children, to limit births. Perhaps both. Certainly, by 1300, the economy of Europe had ceased to grow and population was following suit.

A Malthusian crisis was a serious matter, but the landowning elite further aggravated the plight of peasants before the Great Famine. As economic expansion slowed in the late thirteenth century, many lords, ladies, monasteries, and other landowners needed more cash, and they got it by wringing every last penny out of their manorial tenants. They raised rents and fines; they insisted that all petty fees be paid; they made the most of labor services (especially by converting them into cash rents, as was common by 1300); they sometimes even greedily claimed the fertile manure of their tenants' flocks. These demands left peasants with so little of their own time, goods, and cash that investment and innovation were hard to come by. A Marxist historian might describe this process as follows: the feudal elite extracted so much surplus from the peasantry that the rural economy stagnated. The people of Brigstock knew well what this meant. For example, Margery de Farendraght, a wealthy widow who had leased Brigstock manor from the crown, more than tripled her investment when she subleased the manor to the tenants in 1318. She paid about £13 each year for the lease she held from the king; the tenants annually paid her more than £46 for the sublease. Since the money that went into her coffers did not go into the barns, fields, and equipment of Brigstock, the economy of the manor was correspondingly weakened.

Rising population, declining productivity, and grasping landowners were bad enough, but a fourth factor, the actions of the king, made things even worse. In the late thirteenth century, Edward I began to mount large and expensive campaigns against the Welsh and later the Scots. To finance these wars, he taxed the countryside heavily, and his son Edward II did the same after 1307. Even songs complained about their heavy taxation, one bewailing that "every fourth penny must go to the king." To field large armies, these kings also conscripted young men out of villages and made them into foot soldiers. To feed these armies, they took food from the countryside. Armed with the right of *purveyance,* the king's officers could ride into any village and take away grain, sheep, pigs, fruits, and other produce for the troops. They were not supposed to take so much that a family starved, and they were supposed to leave tallies promising later payment. But hasty officers often left villages bereft of adequate food and adequate compensation. Their arrival was always greeted with dread. Even in 1316, the second and perhaps worst year of the Great Famine, the king's men demanded almost 100,000 bushels of grain and malt from his starving subjects. With taxation, conscription, and purveyance, the king added mightily to the woes of the English peasantry.

So, when heavy rains began to fall in Brigstock in the winter of 1314, they fell on already troubled fields. Cecilia and her siblings probably long remembered the famine that began with those rains, but they had seen trouble enough before. Even when Cecilia had played as a child on the cobbles in front of her house, times were not good. Too many people competed for too few resources; the arable seemed to be losing its productivity; lords and ladies greedily appropriated all they could; and the king took what was left. Whether God sent the rains in wrath or not, England, and much of Europe, was ripe for famine.

THE AFTERMATH OF THE GREAT FAMINE

When the worst of the famine ended in 1322, Cecilia was a grown woman, about twenty-five years old. Her parents were buried in the churchyard of St. Peter, her brother William had returned from his travels with the august title of *magister*, and her other siblings were established in various houses in the villages of Brigstock, Stanion, and Cranford. She was, by 1322, the holder of considerable lands: about twenty-five acres of meadow and three other small parcels of arable. Over the course of the next two decades, she would purchase more land.

The years of the Great Famine, in other words, marked Cecilia's transition from the dependency of childhood to the autonomy of adulthood. When it began, she was a dependent minor in her parents' household; when it ended, she was an independent tenant in Brigstock. The Great Famine did not cause this transition, for Cecilia would have aged and grown in any case. Yet it certainly shaped her young adulthood in critical ways—after all, but for the famine, her parents might not have died when they did, and, but for the famine, she might not have been able to purchase land as easily. In much the same way, the Great Famine shaped the rural economy of the early fourteenth century. As Cecilia tended her lands and flocks in the 1320s, 1330s, and 1340s, she worked in a world that had been deeply affected by the Great Famine.

Uncertain weather continued through the 1320s. In the summers of 1325 and 1326, villages to the south and east of Brigstock suffered from serious drought, a hardship that must have especially embittered those who thought back to the frighteningly heavy rains of 1314, 1315, and 1316. At the same time, the rising sea encroached on arable lands near the coast, causing some communities to lose hundreds of acres to the waves. Cecilia heard about these troubles more than she suffered directly from them, for Brigstock was well protected from the sea and probably also escaped the worst of the drought. Yet stories of parched fields and flooded lands likely confirmed in her mind the wretched uncertainty of the climate. When she examined the clouds in the morning and gauged the wetness of the wind against her face, she must often have worried with a special edge about what the day's weather would bring. In the aftermath of the Great Famine, weather that had once seemed reasonably predictable now seemed cruelly whimsical.

As she trusted less in the weather, she might also have trusted less in her neighbors. People continued to pilfer food and grain with unpleasant regular-

A man threatening a boy who is eating cherries in a tree. Neighborly thefts of this sort grew more common during the Great Famine.

ity; indeed, the unusually high incidence of field crimes reached in Brigstock during the famine did not decline thereafter. For the rest of her life, Cecilia had to guard her sheaves and sheep against theft more carefully than her parents had done. She also had to guard her house with greater care, and perhaps she, like many others at this time, first put a lock on her door, hoping thereby to discourage thieves. Brigstock was not as reliably safe as before. The incidence of bad debts and the animosity between neighbors that they so often produced fell after the famine ended, but then grew in the 1340s to even higher levels. Cecilia seems to have rarely either loaned or borrowed money, but she probably watched as neighbors shouted at each other about misunderstood contracts, unpaid debts, and payments gone awry. This sort of unpleasantness was not new in the fields and lanes of Brigstock, but it was more common than before.

So too were depleted flocks and bad harvests. In 1324–26, Cecilia saw still more sheep and oxen die from another outbreak of murrain. In 1331, 1339, and 1343, she faced again the troubles of a poor harvest. The economy of Brigstock after the Great Famine was fragile, and it seems to have been especially faltering by the 1340s. At that time, more people began to default on debts or sell parcels of land; that is, more people in the 1340s resorted again to the desperate makeshifts that had sustained them through the hard years between 1315 and 1322. The population of the manor followed suit, falling fairly steadily. Where perhaps nine hundred adults had lived in 1300, about seven hundred lived in 1340. (Again, it is not known whether the change was caused by rising mortality or falling fertility—or perhaps even outward migration.) The policies of the crown did not help. When Edward III launched the first campaigns of the Hundred Years War (1338–1453), he began to levy taxes that far exceeded those of his bellicose grandfather in the 1290s. He took, in other words, more resources from a countryside that had less to give. Some prosperity returned after the Great Famine, but it was a lesser and more uncertain prosperity.

THE BLACK DEATH

Before Cecilia died in 1344, she might have worried that the bad harvest of 1343 was the precursor of a new famine. If so, she was wrong. Yet a new danger did await her surviving siblings, nephews, and nieces: plague. Late in 1347, Italian merchants trading with the East brought home fine silks, expensive spices, and a new disease. This contagion killed people quickly, grossly, and without any seeming logic. Some coughed blood and died; some found strange swellings in their armpits and then died; and some survived unscathed. No medicines helped, and no measures, such as appeals to God and quarantines, had any ameliorating effect.[4] By 1348, the Black Death, as it came to be known, had reached England. We do not know exactly when it arrived in Brigstock, for the surviving court rolls end abruptly in September of that year.[5] But it certainly came to Brigstock, probably in the late spring of 1349. Before it ran its course, the contagion killed one of every two or three people on the manor. The plague continued to trouble Europe until the seventeenth century, but its first outbreak in 1347–49 was the most deadly, and its effects were felt for many decades.

In the late fourteenth century, old traditions seemed less secure than before. People began to complain with new vigor about lascivious friars and greedy clerics; peasants found serfdom even more troublesome; rich and poor alike were gripped by guilt about survival, anxieties about the present, and worries about impending death. The despairing spirit of the time was captured in a poem written on the death of Edward III in 1377.

> *Ah dear God, how can it be*
> *That all things waste and wear away?*
> *Friendship is but vanity,*
> *And barely lasts the length of day.*
> *When put to proof, men go astray*
> *Averse to loss, to gain inclined.*
> *So fickle is their faith, I say,*
> *That out of sight is out of mind.*

It seems that the Black Death destroyed more than people; it also destroyed the trust and hope of those who survived.

---

[4]We now know that the main form of this plague, its *bubonic* variety, was spread by a bacillus carried on fleas and rats. Most people were infected when they were bitten by a diseased flea carried by a diseased rat. Since medieval people were unaware of the connection that linked fleas, rats, and human disease, they were unable to combat it effectively. Isolating infected people in quarantines did not help much; attempting to control the rat population would have helped a lot.

[5]Many courts did not keep records during the Black Death and the years that immediately followed, probably because clerks had died or conditions were too chaotic. But it was not the Black Death that caused the surviving court rolls of Brigstock to end in 1348. In World War II, the court rolls were "badly blitzed"; that is, the building that housed them was bombed, and the court rolls for 1349–99 suffered severe water damage from efforts to control the resulting fire. Fortunately, the boxes that held Brigstock's pre-1349 and post-1399 records were not seriously damaged.

Preparing a corpse for burial. The gesture of the person in the middle suggests that the corpse smelled quite unpleasant.

Killing at least one-third of the population of Europe in two years, the Black Death left behind a devastated and often empty landscape. Some villages lost so many people that they were abandoned, their once-plowed fields, empty lanes, and house foundations lying today under the grasses of Europe. Other villages survived, but even they were changed in fundamental ways. The socioeconomic rearrangements that followed the Black Death were complex and slow-moving. In the early decades after 1350, many peasants did well. With low population and plentiful lands, they took high wages for their work and they held lands at low rents. Eventually, serfdom began to decline as lords and ladies slowly found they could better profit from their lands without it and therefore allowed serfdom to die through disuse. The revolts of French peasants in 1358 and English peasants in 1381 were cruelly crushed, but, slowly and surely, serfdom disappeared in Western Europe. High wages, low rents, waning serfdom: these were good changes for the peasantry. But by 1500, other developments boded ill. On the eve of the sixteenth century, many villages were more divided than before by a widening gulf between well-off peasants and their poorer neighbors. And a new danger threatened; lords and ladies, eager to use their land in new ways, began enclosing properties so that they could raise sheep. To do so, they terminated leases and asked long-standing tenants to leave.

Cecilia never had to endure the horrors of the Black Death or the difficult decades that followed. She never saw mass death; plentiful land and good wages; or the enclosures that created, by the sixteenth century, so many landless poor. But it is hard to ignore the devastation that followed so soon after her death. Did the changing times of Cecilia's life contain hints that such a disaster might occur? Or was the Black Death an accidental and external contagion that destroyed a vibrant Europe? If the lives of Cecilia and her neighbors in Brigstock are any measure, the first scenario is more accurate than the second. By 1300, Brigstock was overcrowded and its productive resources were stretched to dangerous limits. In 1315–22, the Great Famine brought more hardship and great devastation. Between 1322 and 1340, unsteady recovery followed the famine. Then, in the 1340s, bad harvests, royal taxation, and other woes further weakened the rural economy. The plague, in other words, did not ravage Brigstock in its prime. When the first plague-bearing rat arrived in Brigstock, perhaps swimming up Harper's Brook or perhaps catching a ride on a cart filled with grain or wood, it found a community already weakened by several decades of hard times.

SUGGESTIONS FOR FURTHER READING

For the two disasters that afflicted peasants in the first half of the fourteenth century, see William Chester Jordan, *The Great Famine: Northern Europe in the Early Fourteenth Century* (1996) and Philip Ziegler, *The Black Death* (1969). See also J. R. Maddicott on *The English Peasantry and the Demands of the Crown 1294–1341* (1975). Edward Miller and John Hatcher provide an excellent summary of the economic circumstances of English peasants before the Black Death in their *Medieval England: Rural Society and Economic Change 1086–1348* (1978).

For debates among historians about the economic and social changes of the early fourteenth century, see Bruce M. S. Campbell, ed., *Before the Black Death: Studies in the "Crisis" of the Early Fourteenth Century* (1991). For a demographic study of a community located about sixty miles west of Brigstock, see Zvi Razi, *Life, Marriage and Death in a Medieval Parish: Economy, Society and Demography in Halesowen 1270–1400* (1980).

For Europe in the aftermath of the Black Death, see especially Emmanuel Le Roy Ladurie, *The Peasants of Languedoc* (1976), L. R. Poos, *A Rural Society After the Black Death: Essex 1350–1525* (1991), and George Huppert, *After the Black Death: A Social History of Early Modern Europe* (1986).

CHAPTER 6

Kin and Household

In September 1319, Alan Koyk transferred a property to his son Richard, and Richard then transferred it to William Penifader. The property is described in confusing terms, but it seems to have consisted of part of a house located between Alan Koyk's main home and the home of William's sister Cecilia Penifader. The house was nineteen feet wide, and it shared walls with Alan's home, on one side, and Cecilia's home, on the other. As stated clearly in the court record, William's acquisition of this house did not entitle him to any use of the farmyard around Alan's home. William Penifader paid the court 3 shillings and 4 pence for this transaction, and Gilbert, son of Galfridus, stood as his pledge.

When Cecilia Penifader was a young child, the kin on whom she most relied were the people with whom she lived: her parents and her siblings. As she grew older, this straightforward situation changed. Cecilia never married, but if she had, she would have added husband, children, and in-laws to the parents and siblings of her childhood. This is what happened to her sister Christina after she married Richard Power of Cranford in 1317 and to her other sister Agnes after she married Henry Kroyl in 1319. Yet even without marriage, the meaning of kinship changed for Cecilia over time, as her parents died, several of her siblings married, and one sister moved away. By the time she was in her early twenties, Cecilia probably no longer lived with kin, and she had added brothers-in-law, sisters-in-law, nephews, and nieces to her pool of relatives. The nuclear kin of her childhood, the parents and siblings with whom she had eaten, worked, and slept, had been partly replaced by an extended kinship network scattered through many houses in Brigstock, Stanion, and beyond. For Cecilia, kinship was always important, but its meaning in her life was constantly changing.

Moreover, while kin were important to Cecilia, so too were the people with whom she lived, whether they were kin or not. Indeed, in Cecilia's time, the Latin word *familia* and the Middle English word *familie* meant a household, not a group of related people. Three things made the *household*—a group of people who lived together, worked together, and ate together—a central part of peasant life in the Middle Ages. First, households were a basic unit of social organization. When the king's officers arrived in Brigstock to collect food for the army or to levy taxes, they took food and taxes from households; when the vicar collected tithes, he proceeded household by household through the parish; when tenants had to agree on when and what to plant in each of the common fields, they met together as heads of households. Second, households were hierarchical places. Every household had a head (most often, a father and husband) who exercised clear authority over everyone. This authority was recognized from without as well as within, for heads of households were often brought to public account for the actions of their dependents. Richard Everard understood this when he complained in 1316 about Robert Penifader and Cecilia taking hay from his fields; he addressed his legal complaint to Robert because Cecilia, who was then a dependent in her father's household, was Robert's responsibility. Third, households were intimate places. People who lived in the same household shared many fundamental things, whether they were kin or not: they used the same bedding and ate the same food; they sweated in the same fields and worried over the same sickly lambs; they hungered together in bad times and feasted together in good; and by the time Cecilia was grown up, they also locked the door of their house against intruders. When Cecilia shared a household with someone, she shared the intimacy of day-to-day life and, at least in the short term, a common fate. Households, which often included non-kin and almost invariably excluded some kin, were probably as important as kinship in the daily life of the people of Brigstock.

KIN AND HOUSEHOLD IN CHILDHOOD

The household of Cecilia's childhood was about twice the usual size. Her mother Alice gave birth to at least eight children and raised six to full adulthood. Most mothers had fewer children, buried more of them in early graves, and saw only three reach maturity. In another respect, however, Cecilia's household was likely to have been typical: like many other households in Brigstock, it was a *nuclear family household*, consisting primarily of parents and their children. Peasants elsewhere lived in different sorts of households. *Stem family households*, households that contained three generations (grandparents, parents, and children), were also common among the peasants of medieval Europe. In some places, especially southern France and Italy, other peasants

A family scene, around the hearth. The mother on the left juggles a toddler while she also stirs the pot. The child on the right uses a bellows to heat up the fire.

lived in *frérèches*, households containing two or more married brothers with their wives and children. In most English villages, however, smaller households were the norm, and most were formed around a nuclear core of husband, wife, and children. Low life-expectancies partly accounted for the nuclear structure of households; since most people died in their 40s, few lived long as grandparents.[1] Housing and settlement patterns also contributed; houses could be built relatively quickly and cheaply, so it was easy to accommodate any grandparent who lived to a great age in a separate house elsewhere in the farmyard or village.

We do not know whether the Penifaders brought servants into their household, but it would not have been unusual if they had. (Servants, like underage children, were rarely mentioned in the Brigstock court. For this reason, we cannot be certain about the presence of servants in the Penifader household, nor can we know whether Cecilia ever worked as a servant.) Whenever the Penifaders needed an extra pair of hands, they had two options: they could hire a laborer to work by the day or task, or they could employ a servant for a year, offering room and board as well as some further reward (in cash or clothing) at the year's end. Laborers were often hired to help at harvest or other especially busy times of year; servants were hired, usually beginning in the late autumn, whenever a household needed help on a long-term basis. Servants were common in Brigstock and elsewhere; in one well-documented village not far from Brigstock, more than a third of households contained a servant.

Most servants were adolescents, learning new skills and earning a bit of money with the hope of someday holding land of their own and perhaps marrying. Associated with youthfulness rather than poverty, service was not demeaning. Poorer households tended to send more children into service, but most servants found that their employers were not much better off than their

---

[1]Although most people died in their 40s, Brigstock and Stanion were not entirely bereft of older people. About 1 of every 10 adults lived beyond the age of 50, and some of these lived into their 70s.

A woman carrying a swaddled child in a cradle. Swaddling kept infants warm and out of harm's way.

parents.[2] Both young men and young women worked as servants, and they worked like everyone else in the household, doing whatever needed to be done. Servants in the Penifader household would have shared its general life, sleeping and eating alongside Cecilia and her siblings, and accepting, like all the Penifader children, the authority of Robert and Alice Penifader. While living in the Penifader household, a servant had a stake in its success; a bad harvest or poor lambing meant a troubled household in which to finish the service contract. The main distinction, therefore, between servants and children came from the link between kinship and inheritance; unlike Cecilia, a servant of the Penifaders could not expect to inherit land or goods from the household. Yet, because inheritance customs favored some children over others, Cecilia could not be confident of inheritance either, and some servants did obtain bequests from their employers. In 1339, for example, Hugh and Emma Talbot of Brigstock arranged for their servant Agnes Waleys to inherit their house and farmyard. Agnes was not related to the Talbots by either blood or marriage, but she had lived with them for at least five years as a valued member of their household. Even in inheritance, then, the gap between children and servants could be a small one.

[2]The practice of sending adolescents to live and work in the households of others was spread through all social levels of medieval society. Among the landowning elite, children were also sent away when they reached their teenage years. Some went to monasteries to begin their training as monks or nuns; some were married young and sent to the households of their new spouses' parents; and many others went to the households, castles, and palaces of family friends where they learned important skills and established social contacts. Some historians have argued that these practices suggest a lack of parental love, but it is just as likely that parental love prompted the practice. By sending adolescents away and encouraging their early independence, medieval parents accomplished two things: they helped their children get a good start in life, and they also somewhat lessened the likelihood of conflict with their adolescent children.

In short, the cramped and smoky house of Cecilia's childhood contained her father (the head of household), her mother, her siblings, and perhaps a servant or two. More than likely, she had other kin nearby (perhaps a grandparent or some uncles, aunts, or cousins), but if so, they lived elsewhere in Brigstock. Cecilia also saw her household expand in some times and shrink in others. Sometimes her parents might have earned extra cash by taking in a lodger or might have provided housing for laborers at the harvest. At other times, her siblings left home either to seek their fortunes elsewhere (as William did in 1308) or to settle in separate houses (as Christina did after she married in 1317). The size and shape of Cecilia's household varied with time, but like most households in Brigstock, it looks surprisingly familiar, with its nuclear core of parents and children, to modern eyes.

Today, it is possible to touch medieval timbers blackened by the smoky houses of peasants like the Penifaders. But there are no archaeological remains, and precious few remains of any other sort, that can reveal whether these houses were filled with love and affection as well as smoke. It is tempting to dismiss medieval parents as unloving and cruel. For example, medieval parents readily beat their children with sticks and boxed their ears. Robert and Alice Penifader would have thought themselves negligent if they had not so chastised Cecilia when she misbehaved, and, indeed, all adults were ready to beat any bad child. For another example, medieval parents put their children to work at young ages. By the age of four, Cecilia would have begun to mingle work with play by watching animals, supervising younger children, and taking on small domestic chores. By the age of eight, when she was old enough to work without supervision, she probably took on a wide variety of simple tasks. In the house and farmyard, she might have helped with cooking, gardening, cheese making, or brewing. In the fields, she weeded, goaded plow-teams, and waved hungry birds away from ripening grain. In the pastures, she guarded sheep against predators, herded them home, and made sure they did not feast in a neighbor's garden. In the woods, she picked nuts and berries, searched out herbs, and collected fallen wood. When we think of a small Cecilia, beaten by her parents and busied by work at so young an age, it is hard to imagine that there could have been much love in the Penifader household.

But the evidence suggests otherwise. To begin with, Cecilia must have been carefully tended as an infant. If her parents had neglected her, she would surely have numbered among the 20 percent of infants who never reached their first birthdays. Most of these children died from diseases that no parent's love could cure, but neglect could quickly hasten healthy infants into their graves. As a toddler, she was also closely watched, probably by her mother or older siblings. Unwatched children tended to knock over pots of boiling water, fall into ditches, or tumble down wells—all deadly accidents that brought on caretakers the censure of neighbors and friends. Clearly, then, medieval parents had to attend closely to their children; if they failed to do so, death or injury was a likely result. By this measure, the Penifaders, with the excellent survival rate of their offspring, seem to have been loving parents.

Moreover, neither child beatings nor child labor meant to the Penifaders what they mean today. First, although medieval children were beaten, so too were adults. Husbands beat their wives; parishioners whipped sinners around the parish church; and corporal punishment was built into the legal system. A miller or baker who cheated clients was put in the **stocks,** a wooden frame into which ankles or wrists (sometimes both) were locked. A cheating **brewster** (that is, a female brewer) faced the dire prospect of the **cuckingstool,** an instrument reserved for the punishment of women; it consisted of a chair set at the end of a pivoting bar from which a brewster would be exhibited to her neighbors and ducked in a pond or ditch. Every manor was supposed to have stocks and cuckingstool, and most people seemed to enjoy throwing rotten food, stones, and clods of earth at those whose misdeeds placed them in either instrument. Second, although Cecilia worked at a young age, neither she nor her parents would have equated child labor with child abuse. After all, Cecilia's work was different from the child labor we now associate with factories in the Third World and sweatshops everywhere. Cecilia worked alongside her parents and siblings, and as she worked, she also played. For Cecilia and her parents (but less so for many modern workers), the boundaries between work and leisure were underdeveloped and fluid. As the Penifaders worked, they sang; told stories; exchanged gossip; and paused for meals, naps, and long rests. As the Penifaders relaxed, they also spun wool, fixed tools, and otherwise finished small tasks. In a world that so mingled work and leisure, Cecilia worked as soon as she was able because everyone worked, and because working was, quite simply, living.

The love that Robert and Alice Penifader felt for their children can be seen most clearly in something practical: their attempts to provide for the future well-being of each child. All medieval villages had customs of inheritance. When a man died, his widow took some of the family lands as her *free bench* or dower, and the rest went immediately to his heirs. Most villages practiced either *primogeniture,* whereby the first-born son inherited the entire family property, or *partible inheritance,* whereby the family property was divided among all sons. Brigstock had its own rather unusual custom that divided the deceased's lands between two sons: the youngest son inherited the lands his father had himself inherited, and the eldest son inherited the lands his father had purchased during his life. All three customs—primogeniture, partible inheritance, and what was locally called the "custom of Brigstock"—preferred sons to daughters. Women inherited only if they had no brothers, and in such cases, *all* sisters shared in the inheritance. Each of these customs of inheritance could leave some children without portions; daughters were usually excluded, and in primogeniture and the custom of Brigstock, some sons were favored to the exclusion of others. What is striking about medieval parents, however, is that before they died, they often took great care to ensure the well-being of children excluded by the strict rules of inheritance.

This was certainly true of Robert and Alice Penifader. They began to provide for their sons early; in 1292, when Robert and William were boys, they held lands for which their parents were primarily responsible. In 1297, the

Penifaders purchased still more land for Robert and William; in 1314, they gave some property to Henry; between 1312 and 1316, they gave lands to Christina on three separate occasions; and in 1317, they probably helped Cecilia acquire her first small properties. We do not know about provisions made for three other children: Emma, Alice, and Agnes. Emma and Alice seem to have died young. Agnes, probably the youngest child, might have received movable goods such as animals, furnishings, cash, or other commodities at the time of her marriage to Henry Kroyl in 1319. (As a rule, daughters were more likely than sons to receive portions that involved goods or cash as distinct from land, and such gifts were rarely noted in the court records now available to historians.) When Robert died in 1318, two of his sons, probably Robert and Henry, were his primary heirs, but he had provided something for all of his living children, except for Agnes, the youngest. By the time Alice died a few years later, she had settled Agnes in a marriage to Henry Kroyl. The generosity of Robert and Alice Penifader toward their children reflected, in part, their relative wealth; poorer peasants gave their children goods instead of land, and still others could offer their children nothing. Yet the Penifaders' generosity also reflects, it is fair to conclude, their careful and loving concern for their children.

KIN AND HOUSEHOLD IN ADULTHOOD

As Cecilia grew up, her household slowly changed in size and shape. By the time she reached her tenth birthday, her siblings were beginning to leave home. William went away to get an education, and Robert and Henry probably moved out once they acquired sufficient lands of their own. In these same years her sisters Emma and Alice seem to have died. Then her sister Christina married, probably a result of long and careful planning by their parents. In 1312, 1314, and 1316, Robert Penifader had gone into court and transferred properties to Christina—first a small plot, then thirty-six acres of meadow, and finally, four small bits of arable land. The next year, Richard Power of Cranford (a village located about seven miles to the south of Brigstock) married Christina. They lived briefly in Brigstock and then moved back to Cranford. Cecilia, probably just reaching her twentieth birthday, was left at home with her father, her mother, and her sister Agnes.

Then Robert Penifader died during the Great Famine, sometime before July 1318. Robert's death left his widow Alice as head of a household that contained herself and her two youngest daughters. She reacted to this new situation in two clear ways. First, she married off one of their remaining daughters; within a year of Robert's death, Agnes was married to Henry Kroyl. Second, she withdrew as much as she could from the usual obligations of a householder; for example, she regularly avoided going to court. Some widows assertively assumed the headship responsibilities vacated by their husbands, but Alice Penifader was not one of these. She settled one daughter in marriage and otherwise sought to be left alone. Cecilia might have stayed with her, perhaps in the house in which she had grown up or perhaps (if Robert or Henry had wanted to move into the old familial home) in another house nearby. In any case, this situation was temporary. Alice lived only a year or so after Robert's death.

For the next twenty-five years, Cecilia lived as a **singlewoman** in Stanion and Brigstock.[3] She was well off, as her parents had left her with some properties, and she later acquired more. Before he died, Robert Penifader had stood pledge for Cecilia when she acquired a small plot and a **rod** of arable from Richard Koyk (a rod was one-quarter of an acre). Before she died, Alice Penifader watched as Cecilia acquired another half-rod, this time from John Tulke. Robert and Alice might have silently financed these acquisitions, and in any case, they left Cecilia with sufficient wealth to purchase still more property. By 1322, she held another rod purchased from Richard Koyk, as well as thirty-six acres of meadow bought from Ralph de la Breche. She acquired still more land in later years.

Cecilia's parents, then, provided her with enough land and capital to sustain herself. They also left her with a supportive network of kin. For example, when Cecilia bought land, she often acquired properties that abutted those of her brothers or otherwise complemented their own acquisitions. When Richard and Alan Koyk were forced to sell land during the famine years, Cecilia and her brother William bought up several of their properties. In 1317, Cecilia purchased a plot from the Koyks that might have lain near a property bought two months earlier by William; in 1319, in the transaction described at the beginning of this chapter, William bought a small house that lay between the houses of Cecilia and Alan Koyk; and in 1322, they separately purchased Koyk land in what likely was an orchard (the field was called *appletrees*). In 1328, Cecilia and William together acquired one-eighth of an acre from Richard Everard. With probably similar intent, Cecilia, William, and Robert each acquired land from John Tulke. Within a few years of her parents' deaths, Cecilia managed properties that lay throughout the fields and meadows of Stanion and Brigstock, but these lands were not randomly scattered. With properties that often lay near those of her brothers, Cecilia could work the land with them—plowing, weeding, harvesting, tending sheep, and the like. She was better able not only to help them but also to seek their help in turn.

Kin were also important to Cecilia when she had to go to court, which as an independent tenant, she did every three weeks. Each time she purchased land or transacted other business in the Brigstock court, she needed a man to serve as a pledge to back up her promise that she would pay the required fine. Most men in Brigstock and Stanion could have done this favor for her, but she usually turned to the same person: her sister's husband Henry Kroyl. Her brother Henry also pledged for her, as did John Kroyl, brother of Cecilia's

[3]Medieval people called a woman who never married a "singlewoman." To Cecilia, our modern term "spinster" would have meant "a woman who spins for a living." The two terms are connected, for many singlewomen in medieval and early modern towns supported themselves by spinning.

brother-in-law; her other pledges were men with whom her brothers had their own separate dealings. In other words, when Cecilia needed help in the court of Brigstock, she relied exclusively either on her brothers or on men well known to her brothers.

Yet although kin were important to Cecilia, she was able to pick and choose among them. Cecilia reckoned kinship, as we do today, bilaterally, that is, ties of kinship ran through both male and female lines. She was an aunt, therefore, to the children of all her sisters and brothers. But she might not have treated these children equally, for she seems to have paid special attention to the least advantaged of her siblings' children—her two nieces (Matilda Kroyl and Alice, the bastard daughter of Robert) and John, the bastard son of William. She treated her siblings with similar discretion. She seems to have spent much more time with her brothers William and Robert than with her brother Henry, and although she dealt often with Henry Kroyl and his brother John Kroyl, she seems to have had no dealings at all with the other Kroyl brothers. For Cecilia, kinship created a *potential* of relationship; in some cases, she developed the relationship fully, in others she maintained minimal contact, and in still other cases, she so ignored a tie of kinship that it did not matter. Kinship was a gentle web with some strong strands and others weak or broken.

In her life as a singlewoman in Brigstock, Cecilia must often have appreciated the support of this gentle web. Her brothers helped her work her lands, and she helped them in return; they assisted her in legal business, as did her Kroyl in-laws; and in the small ways that were so important but so little reported in court rolls, her brothers, sisters, in-laws, nephews, nieces, and other kin enriched Cecilia's world. When she went to church on Sunday, she probably stood with female kin in the nave; when she sat in front of her house on warm evenings, she likely bounced nieces and nephews on her knees; when she walked about Brigstock and Stanion during the day, she might have shared food, chores, and gossip with her sister Agnes and her sister-in-law Isabella (wife of Henry Penifader); when she drank a pot of ale on May Day, she probably told old family stories.

For much of Cecilia's adult life, however, the web of kinship that enfolded her so gently did not extend into joint residence. Many singlewomen, like many widows, lived alone in small houses, and perhaps Cecilia did the same. If so, she might have stayed alone in the house she had shared for a year or so after 1318 with her widowed mother. Since many other singlewomen lived together in twos or threes, it is also possible that Cecilia was able to live with women in circumstances similar to her own. Most probably, however, Cecilia lived by herself, possibly with a servant or two. If so, she was never far from kin. As described in the entry that opens this chapter, Cecilia's unmarried brother William bought a house that shared a wall with her home in September 1319. For the next ten years, he lived next door, perhaps even sharing a farmyard with her.

However she might have lived before, Cecilia's living arrangements seem to have changed dramatically in 1336. In June of that year, she and her brother

Robert combined their resources and probably their households. Robert gave Cecilia his lands; Cecilia gave Robert her lands; they agreed to hold all properties together and undivided. This arrangement suited them well. Robert, like Cecilia, never married, and they were approaching the last years of life. By combining their resources, they supported each other better as they aged, and they also provided more amply for whoever lived longer. According to the agreement, the survivor (it ended up to be Cecilia) was to enjoy the use of the combined properties. Just before Robert died, however, the agreement of 1336 was superseded by a new one. In 1340, he transferred his lands in Brigstock to Cecilia and his lands in Stanion to his illegitimate daughter, Alice daughter of Joan de Lowyk. Cecilia must have acquiesced in this new arrangement. In any case, for several years in the late 1330s, Cecilia and Robert, a singlewoman and a bachelor, combined their resources and created their own household.

Of the six Penifader children who grew to adulthood, William, Robert, and Cecilia did not marry. They were by no means celibate (William and Robert fathered bastards), but they never formed marital households with spouses and children. Although it was unusual for three children in one family to eschew marriage, neither singlewomen nor bachelors were uncommon. Some people did not marry for religious reasons, as was doubtless the case for William. Others were too poor or too mobile to marry; landless men and women who wandered the countryside in search of work often formed informal unions, but they were unlikely to have either the means or the need to marry. Still others might have been deemed unsuitable for marriage, due to physical or cognitive disabilities. Others could have married but did not for reasons about which we can only speculate. Cecilia and Robert fall into this last group. They came from a settled family, they possessed ample lands, they were fully competent adults, but somehow—from choice, procrastination, or disappointment in love—they never took wedding vows.

If Cecilia had married, she would have lived in a different sort of household, and she would have developed different sorts of kinship ties. Her sister Agnes provides a good contrast. When Agnes married Henry Kroyl in 1319, she moved from a household headed by her father into a household headed by her husband. In the first, she was a daughter; in the second, a wife; and in both, a dependent under the authority of a head of household. Agnes and Henry were married for thirty years or more, and they produced two children, John and Matilda, who lived to adulthood. They probably also kept servants in their household, at least occasionally. Agnes, in other words, more or less re-created the household of her childhood in the household of her marriage. Her position changed from daughter to wife and mother, but she spent her life in small, nuclear family households—first, surrounded by parents, siblings, and servants, and later, surrounded by husband, children, and servants. Compared to Cecilia, Agnes' domestic circumstances were much more stable and continuous.

As a married woman, Agnes also differed from Cecilia in her use of kinship. For Cecilia, her brothers William and Robert were important; for Agnes, these brothers seem to have mattered little. When Agnes went to court, the men on whom she most relied were her husband and two of his closest associates, his

The ritual joining of hands at a wedding. Notice how this picture emphasizes the blessing of the priest and how, by adding two attendants to the scene, it also signals the importance of approval by family and friends.

brother John Kroyl and his friend William Werketon. It was almost as if Agnes, having married, redirected her attention away from the Penifaders and toward the Kroyls. To be sure, she certainly visited with Cecilia and chatted with her brothers when she met them in the street, but when she needed help in court, she turned to Kroyls, not Penifaders. Interestingly, Agnes' husband Henry made an equivalent transition. Before marriage, he relied often on his father, but after marriage, he became much more independent of paternal influence. In different ways, Agnes and Henry achieved similar ends: at marriage, they turned away from their natal kin. Their actions underscore how marriage created not just a new household but also, and this is important, a household separate from the parents of the new couple.

Just as we do not know whether Cecilia chose to remain unmarried or was unable to marry, we also do not know whether Agnes and Henry were sweethearts who married for love. Perhaps they were, for they would certainly have known each other from working together in the fields and from relaxing together on feast days. Brigstock and Stanion were too small for them to have been strangers. Agnes and Henry would also not have been strangers to love, perhaps not the courtly love that was becoming so popular among their social superiors, but certainly the companionable love of husband and wife.[4] Some marriages were terrible; Agnes Pole of the nearby village of Houghton-cum-Wyton, for example, was so unhappy in her marriage

[4]Courtly love, in which knights admired and pursued ladies who almost always rejected them, began to be elaborated in the poems and stories of aristocrats in eleventh-century France. It has been called a vicious game, a cult of chastity (since so few relationships reached sexual consummation) and a cover for adultery (since most of the pursued ladies were married). By the thirteenth century, elite literatures throughout Europe had adopted the conventions of courtly love, but it is unclear how readily knights and ladies acted out the behaviors that they celebrated in poetry, song, and story.

that she publicly consorted with her lover and harassed her poor husband. Yet other marriages were affectionate and strong; in Brigstock, the love that one couple bore toward each other was daily recognized in the nickname, Truelove, of one of their sons. Agnes and Henry probably hoped for such a marriage when they married in 1319.

Nevertheless, the decision to marry was not theirs alone. The death of Agnes' father in 1318 seems to have precipitated the marriage, and a substantial land settlement by Henry's parents in 1319 made it feasible. As everyone agreed in the Middle Ages, a good marriage needed much more than the loving consent of bride and groom. First, it needed the consent of parents. Henry's parents arranged for the newlyweds to inherit a semi-virgate of land, and they likely also financed the purchase of a small property (consisting of a house, a farmyard, and six rods of arable land) that was given to Agnes as her dower. Agnes' widowed mother Alice Penifader likely reciprocated by giving the new couple cash and other goods. (In a better recorded marriage in Brigstock, the bride's family contributed an unspecified amount of cash, a cow worth 10 shillings, and clothing worth more than 13 shillings; the groom's parents did as the Kroyls did, giving land to their son.) Second, a good marriage required the acquiescence of friends and neighbors. Friends helped to arrange the Penifader-Kroyl match (Henry's friend William Werketon, for example, stood pledge for him when the Kroyls settled land on the new couple), and friends celebrated with feasting in the aftermath of the church wedding. One such feast in Brigstock cost 20 shillings, more than a year's wages for a male laborer! Third, everyone also agreed that a good marriage required the approval of the Church; in every parish, the parson was expected to publicize the intended marriage to ensure that no impediments stood in the way and, then, to bless the marriage before the altar. So, although the consent of Agnes and Henry was an essential part of their marriage, its full success also required the consent of parents, the approval of friends, and the cooperation of priests. Moreover, had the Penifaders and Kroyls been ordinary serfs instead of privileged tenants of a royal manor, a fourth sort of consent would have been needed—that of their manorial lord or lady.

Agnes and Henry contracted their marriage in a proper and public way, but practice often fell short of the ideal, especially in terms of consent. On the one hand, sometimes young people were married without much regard to their own feelings and opinions. Parents at all social levels sometimes tried to force their children to marry people they scarcely knew, but this was particularly common among aristocrats. When, for example, the Duke of Aquitaine lay dying in 1137, he arranged to marry his fifteen-year-old daughter Eleanor to the heir to the French throne; she had not been consulted, but she duly obeyed. On the other hand, sometimes young people married without consulting their parents or anyone else. For her second marriage in 1152, Eleanor of Aquitaine selected her new husband herself, quickly and quietly marrying a young man who shortly thereafter became Henry II of England. Moreover, although everyone agreed on the desirability of parental approval, priestly supervision, seignorial consent, and community acknowledgment in making a marriage, the Church taught that none of these was essential. A man and a woman could contract a valid marriage by exchanging binding vows in privacy, especially if they followed the vows with sexual intercourse (as usually happened). Couples could be punished for contracting such unions (they came to be called *clandestine marriages*), but the bonds so forged could not be dissolved. Children could and did use clandestine marriage to contract unions of which their parents disapproved. One such case involved Margery Paston, daughter of a Norfolk gentry family, who married her parents' bailiff in 1469, much to the horror of her father, mother, and grandmother. They tried to get the Bishop of Norwich to declare the marriage invalid, but after examining Margery and her new husband about the exact words with which they had exchanged vows, the Bishop declared the marriage a true one.[5]

KINSHIP AND INHERITANCE

In 1344, as Cecilia lay sick in bed, she called into her house three young people: her nephew, John, the bastard son of her brother William Penifader; Robert Malin (who had first come to Brigstock only eleven years earlier); and her niece Matilda Kroyl, the daughter of her sister Agnes. As they stood around her bed, Cecilia gave them a twenty-four-year lease on her lands. In so doing, she effectively disinherited (for twenty-four years) her nearest heir, and she picked among her siblings' children, favoring some over others. Illegitimate children could make no claims of inheritance, but Cecilia chose to favor William's bastard. Girls could only claim inheritance in the absence of brothers, but Cecilia chose to favor her only legitimate niece, Matilda. The biggest puzzle is Richard Malin, for we do not know his relationship to Cecilia. He might have been a nephew born of an illegitimate liaison that is today untraceable; he might have been the lover, fiancé, or husband of a niece; he might have been tied to Cecilia by friendship or service rather than blood. In any case, when these three young people gathered around her, Cecilia sought to manipulate kinship for one last time.

Her efforts failed. After her death, two juries met to discuss the proper deposition of her properties. The first jury judged conflicting claims of inheritance: one made by her sister Christina and the other made by her nephew Martin, son of Henry Penifader. Christina was declared the nearer heir; she and her husband Richard Power took the lands. They immediately transferred about half the land to the disappointed Martin, a move that suggests that an out-of-court arbitration had resolved the dispute by dividing the inheritance between the two parties. A second jury then dealt with the claim of John Penifader, Robert Malin, and Matilda Kroyl to a twenty-four-year lease

[5]Clandestine marriages were outlawed in many European jurisdictions in the sixteenth century, but they remained possible in England until 1753. For more about the Pastons and their exceptionally well-documented trials and tribulations, see Roger Virgoe, ed., *Private life in the fifteenth century: Illustrated letters of the Paston family* (1989).

of these properties. The lease was declared invalid. A custom of Brigstock manor, designed to avoid disputes about deathbed bequests, required that living people who devised land had to be far enough away from death to walk out of their houses. Since Cecilia had not been able to leave her house after she granted the lease, her gift to John, Robert, and Matilda was void. This second dispute had a slanderous edge to it: Cecilia's proper heir (Christina) and the eventual holder of some of her properties (Martin) claimed that the lease was invalid because Cecilia had not been mentally capable at the time of the gift. The jury rejected this claim. In their view, Cecilia had been sound in mind but weak in body.

As Cecilia's kin argued over her lands, her mental health, and her last actions, they acted out the oldest and most enduring story in peasant communities: the story of inheritance, kinship, and land. Cecilia was free throughout her adult life to purchase and sell lands at will, without regard to the claims of any future heirs. She was also free throughout her adult life to use kinship in flexible ways, ignoring some kin, dearly loving others, and perhaps sharing a household with still others. But as she lay dying, these options ceased. The gentle web of kinship had one strand that always ran strong and true: the tie between blood and land.

SUGGESTIONS FOR FURTHER READING

For broad surveys of medieval kinship and domestic arrangements, see David Herlihy, *Medieval Households* (1985) and the anthropological study by Jack Goody, *The Development of the Family and Marriage in Europe* (1983). For marriage in particular, see Christopher Brooke, *The Medieval Idea of Marriage* (1989). For childhood, see Shulamith Shahar, *Childhood in the Middle Ages* (1990). See also the general survey of these subjects for England by Barbara A. Hanawalt, *The Ties that Bound: Peasant Families in Medieval England* (1986).

CHAPTER 7

An Economy of Makeshifts

When the Brigstock court met in March 1317, Cecilia Penifader acquired two pieces of land from Alan Koyk and his son Richard. One was a plot measuring fifty feet along one side (it was carefully measured by Cecilia's brother William). The other was a rod of arable. Cecilia's acquisition of these properties happened in a two-stage process that guaranteed that Richard, the heir of Alan's lands, could never contest the sale. First, Alan Koyk transferred the properties to his son Richard (who paid 2½ shillings for the transfer, using Robert Penifader as his pledge). Then, Richard promptly transferred both properties to Cecilia. She paid 2½ shillings for this final transfer, and Bartholomew de Bekeswell stood as pledge for her payment.

In March 1317, when she was about twenty years old, Cecilia Penifader acquired her first bits of land from Alan and Richard Koyk. She became a landholding tenant, a person with new standing in the community. As a tenant of Brigstock manor, she was thereafter expected to attend every meeting of the manorial court and to cooperate in her use of the common fields and pastures. At this important moment in her life, Cecilia did not act alone. Her brother William measured one of the two parcels she acquired, and her father Robert served as a pledge for the initial transfer. Indeed, her father probably helped her far more than the terse court entry reveals. Perhaps Cecilia purchased these properties with cash she had saved from working as a casual laborer or servant, but her father was probably a silent partner; that is, her parents probably paid for the properties that the Koyks then transferred to Cecilia. Just as the Penifaders had established their other children as landholding tenants in Brigstock, so they also no doubt provided for Cecilia.

For almost three decades, Cecilia held land in Brigstock, and by the time she died in 1344, she possessed extensive properties: a house with a farmyard, more than seventy acres of meadow, more than two acres of arable, and possibly other lands not reported in the extant court rolls. Cecilia held less arable than many of her neighbors, but her overall landholdings were more than enough to support her, provided she worked them well and managed them properly. Moreover, land was not the only resource at Cecilia's disposal. She also had her own labor on which to draw, labor that was defined in part by her gender, in part by her age, and in part by her own abilities. And she had movable goods as well as land and labor. Some of these goods were inanimate objects such as spindles, churns, hoes, tables, and other items found in her house and farmyard. Some were animate stock: sheep, oxen, goats, pigs, chickens, and other animals that yielded such valuable products as meat, skins, milk, and manure. Cecilia was a relatively prosperous woman in Brigstock, but in common with all her neighbors, she had to juggle land, labor, and goods to make ends meet. She also had to be flexible, innovative, and accommodating, prepared to take advantage of any opportunity that chanced her way. In short, she had, like all her neighbors, to make her way in an economy of makeshifts.

THE HOUSEHOLD ECONOMY

Cecilia had to be especially willing to adopt temporary expedients in the organization of her household, the basic unit of her economic life. As a singlewoman, she had to scramble to replicate what her married sisters Christina and Agnes more readily had: the supportive labor of husband and children. This was because Cecilia lived in an economic world structured around households, not individuals. In her day, most people made their livings as members of households, working together for a common profit. Poor singlewomen often found places as servants or lodgers in the households of others, but Cecilia, as a well-off singlewoman, was able to create her own. Still, she could not do all the work of her household herself. Almost every day, she encountered more tasks than she could complete on her own, some of which were considered more appropriate work for men or children than for a grown woman.

As a productive unit, the peasant household had multiple responsibilities. First, the land required constant attention: the arable had to be plowed, sown, weeded, and harvested; meadow grasses had to be cut and dried; pastures had to be carefully watched and maintained; gardens had to be weeded and checked almost every day; fruit trees had to be trimmed and plucked. Second, the animals of the household required a lot of attention, since sheep, pigs, cows, goats, chickens, horses, and oxen needed watching, feeding, and tending on a daily basis. Third, any household that failed to make use of the common areas of Brigstock—especially the woods with its nuts, berries, herbs, and timber, and Harper's Brook with its fish—would have been much poorer than it needed to be. Fourth, almost all foodstuffs required further processing

A woman feeding chickens. Under her left arm, she carries a distaff and spindle for spinning wool into thread.

within the household: grain had to be threshed; meat had to be preserved; milk had to be made into cheese or butter. Fifth, the domestic tasks that kept everyone clothed, fed, and healthy created never-ending work: meals had to be prepared, clothes made and mended, infants nursed, toddlers watched, and the sick nursed back to health or eased toward death.

Most peasant households divided these many tasks among their members according to several different criteria. One division was based on gender. Men worked more often in the fields, and women worked more often in the farmyards around their houses. Although some aspects of this division were determined by biology (only lactating women could feed young infants, for example), other parts were not (for example, nothing biological ordained that brewing was usually the work of women). This gender division of labor was clear but not set in stone. Women went into the fields whenever their help was needed (especially at harvest time, but also to weed, break clods, fix hedges, or even, on a few occasions, plow); men similarly helped with gardening, animal care, or other tasks around the house and farmyard. Both women and men went into the woods around the manor. Women spent much of their time there gathering nuts and herbs; men set traps and hunted. Another division was based on age. Children were given simple tasks that matched their maturity, tasks that gave them more responsibility and took them farther from home as they grew older. At the other end of life, the elderly spun wool into thread, mended clothes, repaired tools, watched infants, and otherwise took on work that was useful but less physically demanding. A third division was based on ability. Not everyone in Brigstock had the strength and experience to plow a straight furrow, build strong crucks for new roofs, or repair a broken plowshare. Most plowmen, carpenters, and smiths were male, and many households hired such men for their skilled help. Most brewers were women (that is, brewsters), and most households bought ale from such women on a regular basis. But even within a household, some people had special skills—skinning animals, making cheese, repairing broken furniture, and the like—that became their own responsibilities. Sometimes these skills divided by gender and age, but not always. When Cecilia lived with her widowed mother, for example, they most likely divided work between them according to whoever made tastier cheese, grew better vegetables, or spun wool more quickly into thread.

For Cecilia's married sisters, the household economy seemed to be almost naturally constituted by marriage. If Agnes did some work, and Henry Kroyl did other work, most of the chores could get done. One medieval song, which tells of a quarrel between a husband and wife, described in vivid terms the complementary work of married couples. The quarrel started when the husband came home to find that his dinner was not ready:

> Then he began to chide and say "Damn you!
> I wish you would go all day to plow with me,
> To walk in the clods that are wet and boggy,
> Then you would know what it is to be a plowman."

For her part, the wife swore back just as vigorously, and she began to itemize the work she did each day: rising early to milk the cows (while her husband, she said, was still asleep); making butter and cheese; caring for hens, capons, and ducks; tending to children; brewing ale; preparing flax; cleaning, carding, and spinning wool. The husband remained unconvinced, claiming that his wife always excused herself "with grunts and groans." Finally, they agreed to exchange chores to determine, by experience, whose lot was the hardest. Unfortunately, the one surviving copy of this song is incomplete, so we cannot know who won this fictional argument, the plowman or his wife. This song seems to anticipate some of the themes we might encounter in a television comedy today: an unprepared dinner; an argument between spouses; an agreement to exchange roles. But in one critical sense, this song is quintessentially medieval: it describes two individuals whose work was profoundly interdependent. Because the plowman went to the fields every day, his wife had grain with which to feed her cows and brew her ale; because the goodwife raised animals and spun wool into thread, her husband had manure for his fields and clothes on his back. Working at separate tasks most of the time, husbands and wives labored together toward a common end—support of their household.

Whenever there were extra tasks to be done, married couples had several alternatives. They could turn to children; they could employ servants; or they could hire laborers, paying them by the day or task. Whenever married couples needed goods they did not produce themselves, they could buy them from their neighbors in Brigstock or from vendors at nearby markets. The household economy matched so well the complementary work of husbands and wives that most men, if widowed, immediately remarried. Some might have done so to assuage loneliness or sexual desire, but the strongest motivation was economic: remarriage was the most practical way to replace labor lost by a wife's death. For many people in Brigstock, marriage or remarriage was the best way to constitute a fully functioning household economy.

Yet it was not the only way. Some people, like Cecilia and her two brothers Robert and William, set up households without ever marrying. Moreover, many widows, unlike widowers, never remarried.[1] If singlewomen, bachelors, and widows had sufficient property, they could maintain their own households, getting the work done without the assistance of a spouse.[2] They managed their households by resorting to two strategies in particular: they relied on kin, and they purchased the labor and services of their neighbors. As to the first, Cecilia never relied on a husband to share with her the work of a household, but she often lived in close proximity to other relatives. In her early twenties, she probably lived for a year or two with her widowed mother; almost as soon as her mother died, her brother William moved next door to her for about ten years; and as she approached her forties, she established a household with her brother Robert. Like her sisters Agnes and Christina, then, Cecilia relied on kin for help and support, but she relied on her mother and brothers, not a husband. As to the second strategy, Cecilia, as a singlewoman, probably used the local markets in labor and commodities with special frequency. Married couples also employed servants or day laborers and also purchased goods, such as ale or bread, from others, but a single householder like Cecilia made especially heavy use of these sorts of opportunities.

THE LABOR MARKET

Some households in Brigstock had more hands than they needed, and other households had too few. The solution was simple: extra hands in one household were employed in another. This labor market operated on three levels: *unskilled laborers* usually worked by the day for a set wage; *skilled workers*, such as carpenters or thatchers, usually worked to complete a specified task (and were paid by the day or by the task); *servants* worked year-long contracts, getting not only room and board within their employer's house but also a specified payment at year's end. By employing all three sorts of workers, a well-off singlewoman like Cecilia completed all the work of her household.

As a female householder, Cecilia faced one particular problem: many tasks, skilled and unskilled, were considered the proper work of men, not women. Men usually plowed the earth, wielded either sickle or scythe at harvest, beat the stalks with flails to separate the edible grain, and did many tasks that a woman like Cecilia usually did not do. How then did Cecilia cope? In part, she probably coped by doing some of the work anyway, for the gender division of labor was flexible enough that some women *did* plow, reap, and

---

[1]It is not clear why women remarried less frequently than men. Perhaps widows competed poorly on the marriage market, especially if they had small children and little land. Or perhaps widows chose not to remarry, preferring their autonomy as widowed heads of household to the dependency of remarried wives.

[2]Singlewomen, bachelors, and widows too poor to establish their own households found employment as servants in the households of others or sought daily work as wage laborers, living as lodgers or alone in hovels. Others pooled resources and lived in common households, of which the best known have been labeled by historians as "spinster clusters."

Men using flails to separate the wheat from the chaff. The freely swinging bar at the end of the flail allowed for more powerful and efficient work. Threshing was usually done during the winter, when the fields and flocks demanded less attention.

thresh. So far as Cecilia had the time and inclination, she could have done these and other "male" tasks herself. In part, she might have coped by calling on the help of her brothers—first William when he lived next door, and later Robert with whom she shared a household. Her brothers, of course, faced a problem that complemented Cecilia's dilemma. They had "female" tasks that needed doing such as gardening, dairying, or herb-gathering. So Cecilia might have helped them just as they helped her. Finally, she also coped, in part, by employing men to do the work for her.

Cecilia probably employed not only local men but also men who passed through Brigstock looking for work. In the early spring, she might have hired a neighbor to plow her few bits of arable land. In the summer, she might have hired some boys to help with haymaking. In the autumn, she might have given a few days' work to some of the men (and women) who followed the ripening grain northward in search of harvest work. Whenever a plowshare broke or her house needed repairs, she turned to a nearby smith or carpenter. More than likely, Cecilia preferred to employ men as laborers, not as live-in servants. Few widows and singlewomen kept male servants in their households, perhaps because neighbors gossiped about imagined (or real) sexual liaisons, or perhaps because women found it difficult to control male servants. Instead of coping with such problems, most female householders found it easier to hire men by the day or task.

Cecilia found these male workers in many ways—by using a smith or carpenter whose skills were well known; by asking neighbors whom she knew needed work; by hiring strangers who stopped at her gate; by looking for strong laborers when she went to market days at Kettering, Geddington, or elsewhere. If she was lucky, she was sometimes able to turn repeatedly to the

Men plowing. The man on the left maneuvers the heavy plow, and the man on the right uses a goad to urge the oxen forward.

same workers, using the same plowman for several seasons, or employing the same harvest workers year after year. If not, she did not need to worry. With about 6 million people in England and not enough land to go around, Cecilia could always find someone willing to work. In the first half of the fourteenth century, laborers, skilled as well as unskilled, were plentiful and cheap.

Cecilia probably made good use of this cheap labor, especially during labor-intensive times of the agricultural year and especially for tasks that were traditionally done by men. But she probably also needed servants to provide steadier and more flexible help. Contracting to live and work with one employer for a year, servants were usually young people who hoped to learn skills and save money. Among young adults, those from poor families were especially likely to seek out such work. Most servants worked for their employers as they had worked for their parents, doing whatever general work needed doing. Although adolescents of both genders worked as servants, Cecilia, as a singlewoman, probably employed female servants only. Perhaps she kept just one servant, but she might also have employed two or more at any time. For the duration of their employment, servants shared with Cecilia the daily life and work of the household. They also lived under her authority. One medieval song tells the fate of a servant who dared to stay out all night. On her way home in the morning, she encountered her angry mistress who shouted at her, "Say, you strong strumpet, where have you been? Your tripping and dancing will come to a bad end!" The mistress then beat the young servant, "over and over again." Good servants could hope for kind treatment; bad servants could expect harsh punishment; all servants knew they had to work hard. Almost every day, Cecilia awoke to more tasks than she could manage. "I have more to do than I may do," was how one woman put it in another medieval song. Servants made it possible for the work to get done. When sheep had to be moved to a new pasture, and fields weeded, and butter churned, and fish caught for dinner, and pigs brought in from the woods, Cecilia did some tasks and left others to her servants.

The day laborers and servants whom Cecilia employed were distinguished from each other by more than the terms of their work. Laborers, whether skilled or unskilled, most often came from the poorer households in

Brigstock. They had little or no land, so the money they earned by laboring was critical in their economy of makeshifts. In Cecilia's household economy, insufficient labor was a major problem; in a laborer's household economy, abundant labor was a major resource. Given her own particular needs, Cecilia mostly employed male laborers, but women also worked for wages. Some laborers were married; some were not. Some were old; some were not. The major characteristic of wage laborers was not gender, marital status, or age, but instead poverty born of insufficient land. In contrast, servants were distinguished more by age than by socioeconomic status. To be sure, the poor were more likely to go into service than the well-off, but this was a slight and inconsistent pattern, especially compared to the strong connection between service and youthfulness. Most servants were young people who hoped, by living as dependents in other people's households, to save some money. Service, in short, was usually a temporary expedient; wage labor was a critical resource that sustained some people over many years.

By paying for the labor of poor neighbors, poor strangers, and young people, Cecilia was able to manage her household economy without the help of husband or children. Just as hired laborers completed some of the work a husband might have done, so servants replicated the work of children. But the labor market did not serve only the singlewomen, bachelors, and widows of Brigstock. Married couples also hired laborers and employed servants, since they too sometimes needed extra help at harvest or regular live-in assistance. Cecilia probably resorted to the labor market more often than did her married sister Agnes, who had husband and children to help her. Yet both sisters, as prosperous villagers with extensive lands and many animals, welcomed at times the hired labor of others.

THE COMMODITY MARKET

Cecilia and Agnes also eased the labor demands of their households by buying goods from others. They were able to purchase almost anything they needed: food, tools, pots, utensils, cloth, leather, furniture, wax, animals. They bought these goods from neighbors, from peddlers or merchants who passed through Brigstock, and from vendors at the weekly markets held in nearby communities. Sometimes Cecilia and Agnes found that it was easier or harder to buy certain goods; during the Great Famine, for example, food was expensive and in short supply, and peddlers were few and far between. But for most of their adult lives, Cecilia and Agnes readily met their household needs by purchase as well as direct production. Moreover, they sold as well as bought. By selling surplus eggs, meat, or wool, peasants like Cecilia and Agnes brought much-needed cash into their households.

Like most medieval peasants, Cecilia and Agnes produced, with the help of kin, laborers, and servants, much of what they consumed. From their fields, gardens, and woods, they gathered sufficient grain, fruits, and vegetables to feed their households. From their flocks and herds, they took skins, wool, milk, and meat for their daily use. In the kilns of Stanion, the center of a small pot-

A woman selling produce to a man who has just pulled a coin from his purse. This sort of small transaction brought much needed cash into many peasant households.

tery industry, they might have fired the pots they used at home. From the quarries outside Stanion, they found stone and rubble for the foundations of their houses, barns, and sheds. Cecilia and Agnes produced these commodities not only for consumption but also for sale—to peddlers who came through Brigstock, to entrepreneurs seeking good pottery or building stone, and directly to consumers at local markets. Many of the foods and goods that peasants sold eventually found their way to urban marketplaces, where townspeople were eager to buy them. Like most medieval peasants, however, Cecilia and Agnes not only produced and sold goods but also purchased them. Some goods were too difficult to find or make in a rural household. Since iron tools could be made only by skilled blacksmiths, cloth-production required looms, and salt could be found only in special locations, these were the sorts of commodities that Cecilia and Agnes sought to buy rather than make. Sometimes, however, they paid for goods that they *could* produce, but only with much inconvenience. Almost all peasant households, for example, were able to brew their own ale and bake their own bread (often using a communal oven), but many chose to purchase these foodstuffs at least part of the time.

The trade in ale offers a good example of buying and selling within Brigstock. Ale was as important as bread in the medieval diet. Because Cecilia avoided water (it was often polluted), turned milk into butter and cheese, and could not afford wine, ale was her basic liquid refreshment. She drank ale every day and throughout the day, not only as an adult but also as a child. As a grown woman, she might have drunk as much as a gallon a day. This does not mean that Cecilia and other medieval peasants passed their days in drunken hilarity. Instead it means that ale had a different function in the Middle Ages than do alcoholic drinks today: ale was, at that time, an essential part of the daily diet.[3] As a result, Cecilia needed to provide herself and the other members of her household with a regular and large supply of ale. When she lived with her brother Robert, for example, they drank about fourteen gallons a week, and since they likely lived with a servant or two, they needed even more.

Producing this ale was time-consuming work. A lot of labor went into preparation: grain (usually oats or barley) had to be turned into malt, with

[3]Nevertheless, Cecilia and other medieval peasants did also drink ale, as many people do today, for relaxation and inebriation. But they separated the weak ales of their daily diets from the strong ales they consumed for pleasure in evenings or at holidays.

several days of careful soaking, turning, and curing; the malt then had to be
ground (either at one of the two mills of Brigstock or with a hand-mill); water
had to be hauled from a well or from Harper's Brook to the brewing site; and
wood had to be collected for a long and hot fire. Brewing itself was also laborious: the water was boiled; then the malt and water were run together into a
kettle or vat; then the used malt was drawn off (and put aside to reuse for a
second, much weaker batch of ale); then yeast or spices were added as the
mixture cooled and fermented. The ale that came from this work was sweet to
the taste (no bitter hops were used in English brewing until after 1400) and
quick to sour. If not consumed within a few days, ale quickly became undrink-
able. For Cecilia and Robert, this meant that they either had to brew ale every
few days or they had to purchase ale from others. For a labor-poor household
like their own, the answer was simple: expend labor on other projects and
purchase ale.

Cecilia bought her ale from local women. Some women offered ale for sale
only occasionally, when their own households could not consume all they had
brewed. Cecilia's mother sold ale in this way, as did her married sister Agnes.
Sales such as these must have been casual and informal; one neighbor would
tell another that she had extra ale, and a deal would be struck. Other sales were
less casual, for some women sold ale as a business venture. These brewsters
clearly relied on the trade to support their households, and although Cecilia
might not have always found ale for sale in a brewster's house, she often did.
In Cecilia's day, about three dozen brewsters worked in Brigstock and Stanion,
but they did not all work at the same time. Indeed, some brewsters sold ale in
one month and not the next, and others ceased to brew for several years but
then returned to the trade. When Cecilia purchased ale, in other words, she occasionally bought it from a neighbor who happened to have extra on hand, but
she usually purchased it from one of several nearby brewsters who, she knew,
often brewed ale expressly for sale. Most of these brewsters were married
women from households of middling status, women with sufficient resources
of labor and capital to make commercial brewing a viable enterprise.

Ale was the commodity most frequently bought and sold within Brigstock. Some households, Cecilia's likely among them, bought most of their ale,
if not all. Some households, Agnes' likely among them, alternated buying ale
with producing it and even sometimes selling off the excess. The poorest
households probably never bought ale at all, either producing their own or
drinking water instead of ale. For some, the ale market was a way to avoid the
laborious work of malting and brewing; for some, it provided a source of
needed income; and for others it was unimportant. The market for other commodities in Brigstock worked much the same: many goods were available for
those who wished to buy them and had the cash on hand. On most days, Cecilia could probably find someone nearby selling bread, meat, fish, wood, or
even a cooked pie. On most days, she could, in other words, supply many of
the needs of her household by purchase rather than production.

Three things are particularly striking about Cecilia's ready ability to buy
or sell goods. First, the commodity market worked reciprocally. When Cecilia

went to Kettering market on a Friday, she went both to sell and to buy. The simple exchanges that happened on market days fed more complex regional and international markets. Cecilia's eggs, sold at Friday market in Kettering, might have eventually been eaten by a monk in Peterborough, and her wool, sold to a woolmonger each spring, might have ended up in the cloth of a Dutch weaver. She, in turn, purchased goods from far away, perhaps dyed cloth from York or salted herrings from the Netherlands. Second, the commodity market emphasizes the importance of cash in the peasant economy. Although some goods were probably bartered for services or other goods, most were sold for cash that was then used to pay rents, buy lands, hire laborers, and, of course, purchase other goods. Third, the strong commodity market of Cecilia's day shows that medieval peasants were neither self-sufficient nor isolated. Cecilia's household economy had to be flexible and adaptable, but it did not have to produce everything she needed. When Cecilia sold some of the wool from her sheep to a woolmonger and spun the rest into thread to sell to a weaver, she was a confident participant in a complex market economy. She sold her wool and thread because she knew she could later buy cloth without having to weave it herself.

THE LAND MARKET

Land was a critical part of every peasant's economy of makeshifts. Whether a household had much, some, or little land determined, in large part, its viability. People in land-poor households could adopt various strategies to get by— such as keeping animals on the common lands, or seeking work as laborers, or selling ale—but none of these could entirely offset a paucity of land. A well-off household had sufficient land (thirty acres or more); a poor household made do with seven and one-half acres or less. Yet thirty acres did not automatically produce a well-housed and well-fed household. Even tenants of many properties, like Cecilia, had to manage their lands carefully to maximize their value.

Cecilia was not always a well-off tenant; over the course of nearly two decades, she purchased, perhaps with the initial help of her parents, the more than seventy acres that she held at her death. She held land, in other words, not because it was family property that had been held by Penifaders since time immemorial, but instead because she was able to take advantage of Brigstock's active market in land. At almost every court meeting, several people in Brigstock transferred parcels of land (usually small parcels of less than an acre) to new holders. As a result, over the course of any single year, dozens of households in Brigstock altered the size and configuration of the lands they held. This does not mean that there was no family attachment to land in Brigstock, but it does mean that the attachment was a weak one. In 1391, a statement of the custom of Brigstock explained that even favored youngest sons might get no family land; they were to get the lands their own fathers had inherited *as long as these lands had not been sold.* Any tenant in Brigstock could, in other words, sell land, even family land that he or she had inherited from parents.

Although Brigstock had an exceptionally vigorous land market, peasants on other manors also bought or sold land, albeit with somewhat less frequency.[4]

Moreover, peasants could lease land as well as sell it. This market is virtually hidden from modern eyes, as leases did not need to be registered in manorial documents. Leasing allowed Cecilia and other peasants to manage their holdings to best effect. Peasants sometimes leased out land that they temporarily did not need or could not cultivate; older tenants, for example, found that this was a good way to keep the security of tenancy without having to work the land. Occasionally, leasing turned peasants into minor landlords or landladies; in one mid-thirteenth-century Gloucestershire village, an enterprising tenant leased land to more than twenty different subtenants! Peasants also sometimes leased out properties as a way of delaying normal patterns of inheritance. Indeed, this was why Cecilia, on her deathbed, tried to pass her lands to John Penifader, Robert Malin, and Matilda Kroyl. If she had managed to leave her house after granting this lease, they would have held her lands for twenty-four years, after which the properties would have reverted to Cecilia (if she had enjoyed a miraculous recovery) or her heirs. Like this deathbed arrangement, some leases were long, but others were short—just a year or two.

Between sales of land and leases of land, households in Brigstock redistributed their landed properties much as they redistributed their labor. One household would sell or lease property it did not need to another land-hungry household. As with the labor market, trade in land was not always a simple matter of redistribution. The well-off could and did exploit the poor. The Koyks might not have needed the land they sold to Cecilia in 1317, but it is also possible that they sold this property as a desperate attempt to raise money for rent, food, or other necessities. If so, they temporarily solved a problem by selling land to Cecilia, but they also impoverished themselves in the long run.

Cecilia seems to have accumulated her land with a clear eye toward its effective management. She held a house and farmyard within which she could raise chickens and pigs, grow vegetables and herbs, keep fruit trees, and otherwise manage much of her day-to-day production of food. She held a few pieces of arable land, some lying so close to the properties of her brothers William or Robert that they might have worked them in common. Most of her land was in meadow or pasture, devoted to animal husbandry. Since animal husbandry was much less labor-intensive than arable farming, Cecilia wisely purchased land appropriate to her situation. With the help of a few servants to watch her sheep and other animals, she could usually manage her lands on her own. She probably only had to hire extra laborers on three occasions during the year: to plow her arable in late winter; to cut the hay from her meadows in June; and to help with the harvest in August and September.

---

[4]It is well to remember that peasants bought and sold their right to *hold* land as tenants, not *ownership* of it. Everyone agreed that ownership rested with the manor, and that peasants were land*holders* and tenants, not land*owners*.

To some extent, Cecilia's lands were an inflexible resource. She had to plant in the fields what her neighbors planted, and she had to pasture her animals according to similar rules. But to a surprisingly large extent, Cecilia was free to manage her lands as she saw fit. She could grow within her farmyard whatever she wanted for her household or whatever she thought might sell well at local markets. She could buy pasture and meadow in preference to arable. She could slaughter some pigs and keep others at pasture. She could lease land for long or short periods of time, and she could even sell her land whenever it suited her (although she never did, as far as we know). Land, like labor, was a critical resource for Cecilia, and, like labor, it was capable of varied and flexible use.

Cecilia was a privileged woman, holding much property and having many kin in Brigstock. Her economy of makeshifts, therefore, can seem to be more a matter of juggling resources than a matter of desperate expedients. Cecilia accumulated sufficient lands to support herself; she managed these properties well; she relied on kin, wage-laborers, and servants to complete the work that her household required; she used the commodity market not only to avoid labor-intensive activities such as brewing but also to make money by selling some of her own goods and produce. Cecilia enjoyed a life that was, by peasant standards, usually prosperous and well-fed. Yet even prosperous peasants were vulnerable to hard times; Cecilia's parents, after all, had died during the Great Famine when ruined crops and sickened animals seem to have hurt almost everyone in Brigstock. Cecilia bought her first bits of land during the famine, so she might have suffered less than most, but this does not mean that she did not suffer at all.

Many of the poorer households from which Cecilia purchased labor, goods, or land faced much more desperate circumstances. Most of Cecilia's neighbors, after all, were smallholding tenants, people with too little land to get by. Like Cecilia, they had to balance labor, goods, and land, but their resources were much more limited. Most had too little land and too many idle hands. For smallholders, the economy of makeshifts was a more unhappy affair, and it would have included expedients—such as occasional hunger, theft, prostitution, and the like—which Cecilia more easily avoided. To some extent, smallholders lived in a complementary relationship with privileged peasants like Cecilia. By working for her or selling goods to her, smallholders made money that helped them survive. But to some extent, smallholders were also exploited by Cecilia and other well-off tenants. In the labor-rich and land-hungry world of the early fourteenth century, Cecilia was able to pay low wages to her laborers and to buy land from the hopelessly poor. In such cases, their desperate expedients were her timely opportunities.

SUGGESTIONS FOR FURTHER READING

Several historians have attempted to estimate how medieval peasants managed to survive with their limited resources. See particularly J. Z. Titow, *English*

Rural Society 1200–1350 (1969), and Christopher Dyer, *Standards of Living in the Later Middle Ages: Social Change in England c. 1200–1520* (1989). For information about brewing in particular, see my *Ale, Beer, and Brewsters in England: Women's Work in a Changing World, 1300–1600* (1996). For information on women's work, see the essays collected in Barbara A. Hanawalt, ed., *Women and Work in Preindustrial Europe* (1986) and Lindsey Charles and Lorna Duffin, eds., *Women and Work in Pre-industrial England* (1985).

CHAPTER 8

Community

In July 1317, Richard Power, who came from Cranford (a few miles south of Brigstock), went to the court of Brigstock and offered to pay for permission "to enter the estate of the lady Queen." In other words, he sought approval to live on Brigstock manor, then part of Queen Margaret's dower. The reason given was a simple one: he was about to marry Cecilia's sister Christina. Permission was granted, payment was waived, and Robert Penifader stood as pledge for his new son-in-law. Richard was then sworn into the tithing of William Pikard.

When Richard Power married into the Penifader family, he could not simply wander north to Brigstock and settle in. To begin with, he had to obtain permission to enter the manor, and this was granted. He then had to establish himself as a law-abiding person, and he accomplished this by entering a **tithing.** A tithing was a peacekeeping group that usually contained ten or more men led by a **tithingman** (in Richard's case, his new tithingman was William Pikard). All men in a tithing were responsible for the behavior of each other. This meant that if Richard had committed a theft after moving to Brigstock, William and the other men in his tithing would have brought him to court for judgment. If they had failed to produce Richard, they themselves would have been liable for punishment. The system of tithings into which Richard Power was integrated in July 1317 was a critical part of peace and harmony within Brigstock. Every year, a special court called a **View of Frankpledge** (frankpledge was another word for tithing) was convened; it not only made sure that all males were properly enrolled in tithings but also punished persons guilty of petty crimes and disturbances.

The presence of tithings reveals some interesting things about the community of Brigstock. First, it was a collective effort. Today, we have police officers to track down wrong-doers. In medieval Brigstock, tithings did the job; friends and neighbors, not officers, had to haul in troublemakers for justice.[1] Second, community was an idea that somewhat respected the boundaries of households. Since every householder was responsible for his or her dependents, wives and children were not in tithings. If children did something wrong, as Cecilia's sisters Emma and Alice did in 1304 when they failed to show up for the boon-work (or harvesting of the demesne), their fathers or widowed mothers answered for them. Third, the community of Brigstock was, in large part, a community of men. All males over the age of twelve were sworn into tithings, even if they were servants or dependent sons. Yet no women entered tithings, even if they were living, as Cecilia Penifader was by the 1320s, outside the authority of a father or husband.

The idea of community is an abstraction, but to the people of Brigstock, it was an important and sometimes compelling abstraction. After all, they had to work together all the time. As manorial tenants, they had to meet the demands of the lord or lady (or raise money to pay their annual lease on the manor). As parishioners, they had to keep the churches of St. Andrew and St. Peter in good repair, as well as meeting other parish expenses. As tenants of lands in the open fields, they had to agree with each other on what to plant, when, and where, and on how best to use fallow lands and the pastures. Within the farmyard of her house, Cecilia could attend to her own business without much regard for others, but everywhere else, she was part of "the community of the vill of Brigstock."[2] She was expected to work with others to common ends.

Those who failed to do so were severely punished. The same court session that allowed Richard Power to enter Brigstock and join a tithing also penalized three men who threatened communal peace and goodwill. William Lori, Robert Lambin, and Peter Kut had so harmed the pastures of Brigstock that their neighbors seized the houses of William and Robert until such time as they would make good on their errors and promise to behave in the future (Peter probably had no house that could be seized). Peter and William were veteran troublemakers; Peter had earlier been involved in a burglary, an assault on a woman, and a nasty confrontation with his tithing, and William was known for eavesdropping on his neighbors, picking fights, and even creating a disturbance during an earlier meeting of the court. It is not clear what these three men did in the fields of the manor in 1317—maybe they released their flocks on a field not yet fully harvested, or let their dogs attack the grazing

[1] In the Early Middle Ages, the peacekeeping collectivity had been kin groups, but by the early fourteenth century, kinship was too diffuse to provide an effective monitoring system. In other words, although there were lots of Penifaders in Brigstock in 1317, they did not suffice to ensure Richard Power's proper behavior. Indeed, it is possible that Richard was enrolled in a tithing that contained none of his new Penifader in-laws.

[2] "Vill" usually refers to a village or township, but in the case of Brigstock, the "community of the vill" (*communitas villae*) clearly embraced the full territory of Brigstock manor, including most of the villages of Brigstock and Stanion.

sheep of others, or put more animals than allowed onto a common pasture. Yet it is clear how their neighbors responded. They told William, Robert, and Peter that they had to leave Brigstock, unless they mended their ways. To Cecilia and her neighbors, community was a powerful idea that sometimes could have real consequences.

MANAGING THE COMMUNITY

With all men over twelve years in tithings and all women and children under the responsibility of their householders, peace in Brigstock was readily maintained. To be sure, problems developed all the time. Cecilia illegally took hay off the land of Richard Everard; she let her animals trespass onto the property of others; she argued with Alice Barker. These sorts of troubles happened not because Cecilia was an especially obnoxious woman, but because problems such as these inevitably arose. After all, the people of Brigstock lived in close proximity, and they bumped into each other and each other's property almost every day. Sometimes it was easy (or tempting) to overlook a boundary stone; easy (or tempting) to let sheep wander onto fresh grasses not one's own; easy (or tempting) to argue with a neighbor about new fences, wandering chickens, or ill-spoken words. When these disruptions occurred, tithingmen and householders made sure that they were quickly resolved either in or out of court. Peace was often broken, but peace was maintained.

The peacekeeping work of tithingmen and householders was not enough, however, to manage all the complexities of life in Brigstock. So Brigstock, like other medieval communities, had a host of officers who ran the manor and its court. The most important was the **bailiff,** the chief officer of a manor. In Brigstock manor, there were usually two bailiffs, one for Brigstock village and the other for Stanion. The bailiffs ensured that Brigstock manor ran smoothly and produced the expected profit. (Depending on who held the manor, this profit sometimes enriched the king or queen, sometimes enriched a lessee such as Margery de Farendraght, and sometimes went to pay the lease or sublease held by the tenants.) Literate men skilled in law as well as business, the bailiffs kept track of payments coming into the manor, as well as manorial expenses. They also embodied the manor to its tenants and to the world. For example, since all land in Brigstock ultimately belonged to the manor (peasants were land*holders* and *tenants*, not land*owners*), land had to be returned to the bailiff whenever it was sold. This is why, when Ralph de la Breche agreed to sell seventeen and one-half acres of meadow to Cecilia in 1322, he went to court, formally returned the land to the bailiff, and then watched as the bailiff granted it out to Cecilia. By thus passing possession of the property through the hands of the bailiff, everyone was reminded that the manor was its true owner, no matter how easy it was for Ralph to sell and Cecilia to buy. In much the same way, bailiffs also acted as the spokesmen for Brigstock manor in the outside world. In 1318, for example, it was doubtless a bailiff of Brigstock who tried to persuade Edward II to lease Brigstock manor directly to its tenants rather than to

Margery de Farendraght. (He failed. Although the tenants offered £50 and Margery de Farendraght offered about one-fourth that amount, the lease went to her—probably as a special favor from the king.) Bailiffs, like parsons, were sometimes local men, but they sometimes came from outside the manor, either minor gentry or prosperous peasants from elsewhere. Everyone was expected to obey them without question. In 1297, for example, when Robert Pidenton and Henry le Leche were elected as bailiffs of Brigstock by a committee of six men, they were explicitly empowered to order the affairs of the manor in any way that they thought best. Of course, Brigstock's tenants, since they usually leased the manor themselves, had an atypical relationship with their bailiffs. On most manors, the manorial lord or lady selected this critical employee.

The bailiff of Brigstock was assisted by other officers, all of them local men elected by the tenants. These officers worked part-time, for they were also landholders in Brigstock, kept busy, like all tenants, by plowing, harvesting, sheep-herding, and the like. The most important officer was the **reeve,** who managed much of the day-to-day business of the manor (again, in Brigstock, there were usually two reeves, one each for the villages of Brigstock and Stanion). The reeve was especially responsible for the cultivation of demesne lands, some leased out to tenants, but others cultivated for the profit of the manor. The reeve had to make sure that these lands were plowed, sown, and harvested on time; that rents of leased portions were duly paid; and that animals were turned onto the demesne in proper numbers at proper times. The reeve supervised the **haywards,** who kept track of what went on in the fields and flocks of the manor. Bailiffs, reeves, and haywards worked together to make sure that the arable fields and pastures of Brigstock were well and honestly used. Sometimes they also made mistakes. In 1306, for example, the bailiff of Brigstock accused Robert Penifader of letting his animals feed illegally on the demesne. Robert vigorously denied the accusation and found six men willing to swear to his innocence. He was then acquitted of the charge. But the haywards who had originally raised the accusation with the bailiff were then charged with doing their job so poorly that an innocent man had been falsely accused.

The harvest, with villagers carrying and stacking sheaves. During the harvest, neighbors often cooperated with one another to bring in the crops as efficiently as possible.

Three other sorts of officers did their most important work when the court of Brigstock convened every three weeks. *Jurors* served on an ad hoc basis, selected whenever a **jury** was needed, and they had two functions: reporting wrongdoing and judging cases. The first function is less familiar today, but then it was very important. Because reeves, haywards, and other officers inevitably overlooked some misdeeds, *juries of presentment,* as they were called, reported wrongdoers who might otherwise have been missed. Hence, at the end of every View of Frankpledge in Brigstock, a jury judged whether the officers of the manor had presented all misdoings properly; if not, the jurors could add to or emend the charges.

The second function of juries, judging special cases, helped to resolve arguments within Brigstock. For example, when Cecilia's kin argued fiercely over her inheritance in 1344, the matter was settled by *trial juries* rendering firm verdicts. Christina and her nephew Martin disagreed about who was Cecilia's nearest heir, and they jointly opposed Martin's cousins who claimed that Cecilia had granted them a twenty-four-year lease. Who was Cecilia's nearest relative? Was she of sound mind when she granted the lease? These are the sorts of questions that could and did create enduring enmities, and, in some such cases, the process of judgment by jury helped to calm things. In the dispute between Christina and Martin, twenty-four men were selected and sworn to serve as jurors; they talked among themselves about the inheritance customs of Brigstock and how they applied to Cecilia's survivors, and they rendered a legal verdict. They probably also did more than merely judge, for when they awarded the inheritance to Christina, she promptly transferred a good part of it to Martin. This suggests that the formal verdict of the jury was accompanied by informal arbitration; in other words, the jury both rendered a legally binding verdict and facilitated an equitable resolution that went beyond the strict dictates of law. Whether jurors arranged this extra-legal resolution or not, the process of judgment by jury—friends, neighbors, and coworkers who gathered together to talk through the facts—could help to resolve disputes and cool tempers. Resolution was not, however, guaranteed. In the dispute that pitted Christina and Martin against Cecilia's lessees, the twelve men selected as jurors offered a straightforward judgment: the lease was invalid. Christina and Martin were doubtless pleased, but Martin's cousins, who thereby lost a lucrative lease, probably left court thinking that they had been cheated of a good deal and blaming their loss on the men who judged against them. Whether presenting or judging, juries were composed of local men drawing on local lore. They based their determinations on custom (for example, their understanding of how nearness of kinship was figured in Brigstock) and on knowledge of local doings (for example, their information about whether Cecilia had or had not left her house during the last days of her life). Unlike modern jurors who are, ideally, uninformed and open-minded about a case, medieval jurors were expected to be informed, knowledgeable, and even opinionated about the cases before them.

Court business was completed with the help of two other officers. **Aletasters** supervised the brewers of Brigstock, making sure that they sold good quality ale at fair prices and fair measure. The work of an aletaster might sound delightful to some, for (as the title implies) he was expected to taste each batch of ale before it was put on sale. But an aletaster had a hard job. He had to be ever-vigilant against the cheating schemes of brewers, and he also sometimes had to taste ale that was sour or even unhealthy. In many places, he also was supposed to oversee the trade in bread, checking to be sure that bakers sold bread that was good quality, proper weight, and fairly priced. Aletasters were kept very busy. Usually there were two aletasters working in Brigstock village and another in Stanion. Every three weeks, these men stood before the court of Brigstock and announced the results of their ongoing supervision, naming all brewers and specifying their misdeeds, if any.

Affeerors had a single but important function: they determined how much money had to be paid for each reported action or offense. Almost every transaction in court resulted in a payment of money—money paid to transfer land, money paid to resolve a dispute between neighbors, money paid by brewers (even honest ones) to practice their trade, and money paid as punishment by wrongdoers. Affeerors determined how much would be due from each person for each transaction. They seem to have based their judgments partly on the nature of each transaction (Was the offense grievous? Was a particularly valuable piece of land being sold?) and partly on the ability of people to pay. Fines for poor people were often forgiven, and fines for everyone were sometimes reduced in hard times. For example, brewers' fines fell rapidly during the Great Famine and somewhat more slowly thereafter. The most likely explanation is that the affeerors of Brigstock, well aware of how hard times were afflicting everyone, assessed lower sums.

All of the officers who helped to manage the community of Brigstock were men; no woman ever served as bailiff, reeve, juror, or even aletaster in Brigstock. For Cecilia, this one aspect of community life was closed to her. This was true elsewhere too, for with a few rare exceptions, peasant women did not hold manorial offices. The officers of Brigstock were also prosperous people. Well-off families in Brigstock repeatedly produced most of the manor's officers, and poorer families usually produced none. The system was largely self-perpetuating. The Brigstock court rolls say that officers *electi sunt* ("were elected"), but in some cases, this clearly meant that a committee of six or twelve men (probably former officers) selected new officers. About one-third of the households in Brigstock boasted a man who at least occasionally held office, and the Penifaders were among them. Cecilia's father Robert served at various times as an aletaster, a juror, and an affeeror. Her brothers were less active: Robert served only twice as a juror; Henry never held office; and the same was true of William (who, as a cleric, would have been passed over for such work).

Bailiffs were usually paid directly for their work, but reeves, haywards, jurors, aletasters, and affeerors often worked without direct compensation. Why did men serve? In part, they served because of the indirect profits of their offices. In Brigstock, as elsewhere in medieval Europe, an office was a responsibility, but it was also a source of income. Officers were expected to receive gifts or even collect fees from those they helped, to gain advantages from insider knowledge, and to profit from all sorts of special favors. In part, however, men served because they were expected to do so. In Brigstock and elsewhere, social prominence brought social responsibility; well-off men were expected to help govern their communities. Sometimes peasants sought to avoid official duties, but such efforts were rare and discouraged. In 1314, for example, the affeerors of Brigstock determined that Cecilia's father had to pay the considerable fine of twelve pence if he wished to be excused from the office he was then holding. Robert Penifader thereby avoided the duties of his office, but he paid dearly for his exceptional exemption.

Householders and tithingmen helped to maintain the peace; bailiffs, reeves, and haywards kept the manor running in good order; jurors, ale-tasters, and affeerors completed much of the crucial business of the three-weekly court. They were kept busy because arguments, disagreements, and petty crimes were daily occurrences in Brigstock. At every three-weekly meeting of the Brigstock court, people arrived to register complaints and resolve disputes. In January 1343, when Cecilia Penifader and Alice Barker brought their argument to court, other problems from recent weeks were also on the agenda: John, son of John Thomason, filed a complaint against John Golle; John Colbeyn entered a similar plea against Richard Chotty; Robert de Albathia was named for letting his horse wander into the west pasture; the executors of John Hirdman's estate settled an argument with John dil Sik; Richard Swargere and Isabel, daughter of William Golle, agreed to end a long-standing quarrel; Hugh Golle, John Golle, and William Miller were cited for letting their pigs loose near the millpond; and Robert ad Stagnum came to court to complain of a trespass made against him by John Stratton. There was also a lot of petty crime in Brigstock. Serious crimes had to be taken before the king's justices, but petty crimes were reported at the annual View of Frankpledge. At the View held in 1343, for example, it was reported that people in Brigstock had attacked officers, robbed houses, moved boundary markers, harbored strangers, thrown dung into the street, obstructed the road with new buildings, cheated their neighbors by selling bad goods, and drawn blood in fights. Many of these crimes were first reported by the raising of a **hue.** If anyone came upon the scene of a crime, they were to shout loudly (that is, raise a hue), and everyone within earshot was to run to their aid. The hue must have been commonly heard in the fields and lanes of Brigstock; almost every week, someone was doing something wrong.

As they took care of the administration of Brigstock—managing its manor, settling its disputes, and punishing its crimes—the officers were guided by its *customs* and **by-laws.** Like all peasants, the people of Brigstock had their traditional or customary ways of doing things. The best example is the "custom of Brigstock," which divided a deceased man's lands between his eldest and youngest sons. Customs guided the actions of all. When a reeve had to decide whom to call into the fields or a hayward had to determine whose sheep should be pastured where, they could use custom to guide their decisions. What had been done in the past could reasonably be done again. For example, a jury in 1304 was convened to determine customs about boon-works on the demesne at harvest time; they reported that all persons living on the manor had to perform boon-works, but those few people in Brigstock and Stanion who lived on properties not part of Brigstock manor were free of this obligation. Like other peasants, the tenants of Brigstock supplemented custom by agreeing on new rules or by-laws that they would observe. In 1337, for example, the tenants agreed on new guidelines for the harvest: no one was to take sheaves off the fields; no one who was healthy enough to work as a wage-laborer was allowed to glean behind the harvesters; and no one was to leave Brigstock during the harvest to seek work elsewhere. In the gap between customs and by-laws, medieval peasants often "invented tradition," developing new rules that they quickly accepted as practiced "time out of mind," and that they sometimes even justified as merely strengthening traditional practices. In any case, the numerous officers of Brigstock had heavy responsibilities, but they did not act according to whim. At every turn, they were guided by the long-standing customs and the more recent by-laws of the community.

FRIENDS AND NEIGHBORS

Whenever Cecilia stood upright on hot August afternoons to rest her tired back from the labor of the harvest, she saw the fields around her filled with the people of Brigstock. She knew them all, even if she knew some better than others. Indeed, save for a few laborers who had come to Brigstock to find employment at harvest time, Cecilia saw people she knew intimately: her family, her friends, her neighbors, and her fellow tenants at work. To an outsider—to a lord who might have cantered by, or even to us, if we could have stood and stretched with her—the field would have seemed full of humble peasants, all very much the same. Some were young or old, some were male and others female, some were mowing grain while others bundled and stacked it, but they were all *peasants*. Cecilia saw things differently. To her, the peasants of Brigstock were not all the same. Some were well-off, and others were not. Some had been born in Brigstock, and others were more recently settled in the community. These socioeconomic differences privileged Cecilia, who had been born into a prosperous local family, but they left others in more vulnerable circumstances.

Because no complete rentals or tax listings survive for Brigstock in Cecilia's day, the Penifaders' circumstances cannot be precisely estimated or even ranked within the community. Cecilia's parents, Robert and Alice, were relatively well-off, but we do not know exactly how much land they held. For only one Penifader can we confidently state the full extent of his landholdings. In 1326, a few years before he died, Cecilia's brother William transferred his properties to his bastard son John. His grant carefully specified twenty separate units, which totaled up to a house (located next to Cecilia's house), a couple of acres of arable, and almost one hundred and forty acres of meadow and pasture. Cecilia's landholdings were smaller but certainly comparable in terms of the balance between pasture and arable: over the course of her life, she ac-

A woman sitting on a bench, with a bowl at her feet. Benches were much more common than chairs, and they were used both indoors and outdoors. Cecilia, like most peasants, probably spent many hours sitting on a bench in front of her cottage.

quired more than seventy acres of meadow and pasture along with about two acres of arable land. By the standards of the day, William and Cecilia held a great deal of land, even if mostly pasture. The Hundred Rolls, a survey of English landholding taken in 1279, suggest that land was distributed among the peasants of England as follows:

Tenants of 30 acres or more:	26%
Tenants of 15 acres:	32%
Tenants of 7½ acres or less:	42%

The Penifaders were among the most privileged of peasants, holding much more land than most.

How much land did a family need to survive? The answer depends on terrain, soil, and economy. In the midlands region where Brigstock lay, a husband, wife, and three children were prosperous—by peasant standards—if they had thirty acres or more of land; in a good year, they could take from thirty acres more than they needed to consume themselves. With the surplus they sold, they could repair their house, buy more animals, fix a plow, or otherwise improve their circumstances. Only one in four peasant families was this fortunate, but the Penifaders were among them. Rather more numerous were middling families who had to get by on about fifteen acres of land. With luck and some economizing, fifteen acres could just support five people, but with no room for extra expenses and no surplus. Whenever misfortune came—rains ruining a harvest, a wife breaking her leg, a cow dying from inexplicable illness—middling families fell into debt. Yet even they were more fortunate than the smallholders who predominated in most villages. Families of five could not be supported by holdings of 7½ acres or less, so these tenants had to supplement fieldwork with nonagricultural sources of income. Some worked as thatchers, carpenters, charcoal-makers, potters, clothworkers, smiths, or brewers; others hired themselves out as general laborers to their neighbors; all took advantage of whatever they could find in their ongoing economy of makeshifts. Still, with their small bits of land, smallholders were better off than the landless. With nothing but their labor to support them, landless men and women (and sometimes children too) wandered about the countryside seeking work and charity.

In communities like Brigstock, then, there were some families that ate well after a good harvest, some that ate more cautiously, and some that ate with hunger always at the table. Some families were well-housed with shuttered windows and high roofs to draw off the smoke; some had more simple houses that nevertheless offered sturdy protection from the elements; some made do with hovels that were too easily invaded by wind, rain, and damp. The standard of living in medieval villages, in other words, was sometimes good, often adequate, and most often poor.

These differences affected more than just housing and food. Prosperous peasants like the Penifaders essentially ran their communities as they liked. Holding thirty acres or more, well-off families had considerable economic power over their neighbors. The Penifaders were able to offer fieldwork to their less fortunate villagers; they paid for the services of carpenters, thatchers, and brewers; they offered loans; and perhaps most important, they bought the lands of those fallen on hard times. Tenants of large properties also predominated among officeholders, giving them considerable political power; when Robert Penifader served as a juror, aletaster, or affeeror, he was able to manage the affairs of the manor as he, and his equally prosperous colleagues, thought fit. The economic and political powers of well-off peasants were further enhanced by social advantages. Prosperous tenants associated mostly with each other to the exclusion of those less privileged, and they also predominated among the families settled permanently in Brigstock. Finally, well-off peasants even had a demographic edge over their lesser neighbors: they not only had larger families (as did the Penifaders) but also enjoyed a good chance of living longer and healthier lives. To be born a Penifader in late thirteenth-century Brigstock was to be a very fortunate peasant.

But to be born a Penifader did not guarantee a prosperous life. What one generation had, the next could soon lose, so that distinctions between well-off, middling, and poor rarely extended over many generations. Sometimes a couple produced no offspring in the next generation; sometimes children survived but did not do as well as their parents; and sometimes some siblings managed better than others. William and Cecilia did well enough to maintain the prominent place that their father and mother had enjoyed, but their brothers Robert and Henry seem to have led much more modest lives. Similarly, Agnes Penifader's husband Henry Kroyl followed in his father's footsteps as a prominent villager, but two of his brothers were much less fortunate men. It is easier to see these patterns than to explain them. Sometimes parents discriminated between children, setting some up nicely and leaving others to fend more for themselves. Yet in other cases, the distinctions that arose among siblings or between generations seem to have resulted from luck, personality, or both. The important point, however, is that there were no longstanding dynasties among peasants. In any generation, some households were better off than others, but few families were able to sustain such dominance over many generations. This was as true of the Penifaders as of others. Robert and Alice Penifader led prosperous lives, as did most of their children, but 100 years later, only a few Penifaders still lived in Brigstock and Stanion, and they scraped by in more modest circumstances.

A LOSS OF COMMUNITY SPIRIT?

The community of Brigstock actively governed itself and disciplined its wrongdoers, but it was not homogeneous. Compared to her many desperately poor neighbors, Cecilia enjoyed a comfortable life. She had much land, good housing, and abundant food. Cecilia also enjoyed more social and political influence than did most people in Brigstock. Many of her neighbors had little to say about how the manor was managed, but through her father Robert, her brother Robert, and her brother-in-law Henry Kroyl, Cecilia had access to some powerful local men. And Cecilia was rooted especially deeply in her community. Many of her neighbors had to leave family and kin behind as they migrated in search of better opportunities, but Cecilia died where she had been born, always surrounded by kin. Cecilia was, of course, just a peasant, and to an elite lady or an urban silkworker, she might have seemed a laughably poor countrywoman. She also had some neighbors who were better off and more influential than she. But all in all, Cecilia enjoyed a more secure and prosperous life than did many of the other people in Brigstock.

In terms of the reality of community within Brigstock, it matters a great deal that most of Cecilia's neighbors were much less fortunate than she. The people of Brigstock cooperated with each other almost every day, and they were capable of evoking with great feeling the idea of community. Yet their communal solidarity was undercut by the poverty of some and the prosperity of others. These differences caused anger, resentment, and crime; in most villages, burglaries and assaults were most frequently perpetrated by poor peasants against their well-off neighbors. Hard times worsened these tensions. When petty crimes doubled in Brigstock during the Great Famine, poorer peasants desperately resorted to theft to feed their families, and those better-off sought just as desperately to protect what seemed rightfully theirs. When bad debts increased, resentments built between poor debtors and unpaid lenders. When the pace of land sales quickened, well-off peasants benefited from the hopelessness of the poor. Cecilia might have often looked at her poor neighbors with feelings of pity, exasperation, and expectation; she gave them charity and help, but she also employed them, loaned them money, and bought their land. They probably looked at her, in turn, with envy, deference, and anger; they needed her assistance and employment, but they also resented her privilege and readily pilfered from her.

We should also remember, in trying to assess what community really meant to Cecilia and others, that Brigstock was a community of many overlapping jurisdictions. It was a manor that messily spanned most (but not all) of the villages of Brigstock and Stanion and that took in small bits of the two nearby villages of Islip and Geddington. It was a parish that fully encompassed Brigstock and Stanion, but had no part of worship in Islip or Geddington. It was two villages, joined closely but imperfectly by settlement history, manorial structure, and parochial administration. Sorting out what "community" meant across these jurisdictions was sometimes a difficult business. For example, the jury that discussed boon-works in 1304 had to distinguish among (a) tenants of Brigstock manor in the villages of Brigstock and Stanion, (b) men in the tithings of both villages, and (c) persons who lived in Stanion and Brigstock on some of the few tenements not part of Brigstock manor. Sometimes a person was part of the community (for example, in a tithing) but also outside it (for example, not a tenant of Brigstock manor).

Moreover, Brigstock was not an island, isolated from external influences. Every day, people walked out of Brigstock to visit relatives, sell goods, and seek work, returning again by sunset. Every day, people came to Brigstock for exactly the same reasons. When Christina Penifader moved to the original home of her husband Richard Power a few years after their marriage, Cecilia probably thought little of walking to Cranford for a visit and then returning the same day. Cecilia probably also thought just as little about the long-term migration that brought some people to settle in Brigstock and took others away. Like Richard Power, people moved to Brigstock, married local people, bought land, and sought work. Like Richard Power, some moved on in a few years, and others stayed put. For Cecilia and everyone else in Brigstock, daily movement and long-term migration created communities bigger than Brigstock—a community of day-to-day movement that embraced a circle extending about fifteen miles from Brigstock and a regional community that covered the English Midlands. As Cecilia and her neighbors traveled along the roads and paths that surrounded their manor, they moved within a broader community of villages and towns that regularly exchanged goods, people, and services.

It is possible, as some historians have suggested, that the powerful ideal of the "community of the vill" declined after the Black Death. Some communities were wiped out by the plague. Those that survived seem to have been under particular stress in the late fourteenth and fifteenth centuries. Men increasingly refused to serve in manorial offices; by-laws became more strident and restrictive; legal forms of cooperation among peasants declined. Perhaps such changes show a waning of community spirit, but perhaps not.[3] We can, however, be sure of one thing: there is no reason to wax nostalgic about the "com-

---

[3]For example, it is hard to know whether the proliferation of by-laws in the fifteenth century suggests a stronger community (which therefore articulated its practices more fully) or a weaker community (whose unwritten practices had to be strengthened by written record). Moreover, it is possible that by-laws multiplied after the Black Death for reasons that relate not at all to the waxing or waning of community spirit—perhaps, that is, by-laws proliferated in response to such factors as new seigniorial interests or new agricultural practices.

munity of the vill" in Cecilia's day. Some people imagine that a sense of community was better achieved in past times—that it was free of conflict, strengthened by homogeneity, and purified by isolation. This is a fantasy. Cecilia's experience of community was much like ours: powerful and compelling in conception, fractured and partial in reality.

SUGGESTIONS FOR FURTHER READING

Some of the best illustrations of community life in the medieval countryside come from studies of specific places. There are many of these, but see especially Emmanuel Le Roy Ladurie, *Montaillou: The Promised Land of Error* (1978), and Edwin Brezette DeWindt, *Land and People in Holywell-cum-Needingworth: Structures of Tenure and Patterns of Social Organization in an East Midlands Village, 1252–1457* (1972).

For more information on by-laws and rural self-government, see Warren O. Ault, *Open-Field Husbandry and the Village Community: A Study of Agrarian By-Laws in Medieval England* (1965). For incomes and budgets of well-off, middling, and poor peasant households, see Christopher Dyer's *Standards of Living in the Later Middle Ages: Social Change in England c. 1200–1520* (1989).

CHAPTER 9

Women and Men

In June 1336, Cecilia's brother Robert went to the Brigstock court and "delivered, granted, and sold" his land to her. After Robert stipulated that he would keep for himself half of the proceeds from the land, the clerk noted that Robert and Cecilia would hold the property undivided. Immediately afterwards, Cecilia stood before the court and "delivered, granted, and sold" her properties to her brother. Like him, she stipulated she would retain half of the proceeds from the land, and it is also likely that the clerk again wrote that Cecilia and Robert would hold these properties undivided (if so, this stipulation is lost in the frayed and torn edge of the court roll that survives today). By these two transfers, Cecilia and Robert merged their properties into a combined unit.

When Cecilia Penifader and her brother Robert stood before the court of Brigstock in June 1336, they acted as two equally competent adults. Both were tenants of the manor, both freely disposed of their lands, and both transferred their properties under identical terms. Cecilia was a woman and Robert a man, but it seems that, in this instance, distinctions of gender did not matter. What Cecilia and Robert did in June 1336, their married brother Henry could also do. That is, Henry too could transfer without restriction any lands that he held by right of sale, gift, or inheritance. Yet the two Penifader sisters who married, Agnes and Christina, were not capable of doing what their brothers and unmarried sister did so easily. That is, Agnes and Christina, as married women, could not sell or give away land, unless they had the express permission of their husbands. This was because, as a Brigstock jury baldly put it in 1315, "A wife's sale is nothing in the absence of her husband." Both married

Penifader sisters acquired lands in their own right, by gift (in Agnes' case) and by purchase and inheritance (in Christina's). Agnes and Christina later sold these lands. In both cases, they could only do so with the approval of their husbands, who stood at their sides when they came to court to register the sales.

The experiences of Agnes and Christina reveal an important fact about the status of married women in Brigstock and other medieval communities: they were not treated by their courts as full adults. A wife was a dependent of her husband, the acknowledged head of their household. In public, he answered for the household, accepting responsibility for the misdeeds of its members, managing its real or movable property, and expressing its interests whenever villagers met to discuss the open fields and common pastures. In private, he also wielded real authority, for, as head of household, he possessed the unquestioned right to manage the household economy as he saw fit and to discipline his wife, children, and servants. Henry Kroyl might have been a loving and kind husband who never raised his hand against Agnes Penifader and always listened carefully to her advice. Yet Henry was not *required* to be kind, loving, and attentive. If he sold land despite Agnes' protests, or wasted their money on strong ale, or beat her regularly, Henry would not have exceeded his acknowledged authority as head of their marital household.

Cecilia Penifader provides an interesting contrast to the respective roles of her sister Agnes and Agnes' husband Henry. Cecilia and Agnes shared some important disabilities that sprang from their gender. After all, as women, they could not join tithings, could not usually act as pledges in court, and could not serve as manorial officers. Yet for most of her adult years, Cecilia behaved, in some respects, more like her brother-in-law than like her married sister. Like Henry, Cecilia went to the court as a full and autonomous tenant. Like him, she made critical decisions that affected the welfare of her household and its members. Like him, she would not have hesitated to discipline her servants if she saw need. Cecilia was a woman, but she was also a head of household, and therefore, she was able to do many things her married sister could not. In Brigstock, differences of gender profoundly shaped the lives of women and men, but so too did differences between householders and dependents.

GENDER RULES IN CECILIA'S WORLD

At every moment of her life, Cecilia lived in a world that clearly and firmly distinguished between female and male. Even the first moments of life were a gendered experience, for childbirth was women's work from which men were banished. Alice Penifader labored to bring forth each of her eight children in the main room of their house (or perhaps in a small room off to the side); she rested on bedding, paced on the packed dirt floor, and tried to speed the birth by squatting, possibly on a birthing stool. In her labor, she was assisted by other women, including female kin, friends, and neighbors. One of these might have been a midwife, a woman locally known for her skilled assistance at births. Sent into the farmyard or perhaps to a nearby house, Robert Peni-fader and the Penifader children had nothing to do with this mysterious and woman-dominated business. The same was true of the churching ceremony that followed every safe delivery. Six weeks after she gave birth to Cecilia and each of her other children, Alice went to church to give thanks. This happy occasion was as gender-segregated as childbirth since, except for the priest and his assistants, men stayed away from churchings. Each time she went to be churched, Alice was congratulated and praised by the female kin, friends, and neighbors who had helped to bring her safely through labor.

Born into a family that already boasted several brothers and sisters, Cecilia seems to have been welcomed and loved by her parents. But sons were preferred. After all, it was to sons that the most important household lands might someday devolve. English peasants practiced many customs of inheritance, but all of these customs favored sons—either oldest sons, all sons, youngest sons, or, as in Brigstock, the oldest and the youngest sons. English peasants also sought to provide for children excluded from inheritance, but in so doing, they were not egalitarian. Noninheriting sons were more likely to get a bit of land from their parents; noninheriting daughters were more likely to get movable goods, such as cash, animals, or other commodities.[1] Robert and Alice Penifader probably loved all their children, but they also knew that the link between family land and family name ran through males only. Although the active land market of Brigstock made this link somewhat tenuous, it was not altogether severed. Did such concerns affect the care with which the Penifaders nurtured their daughters, as opposed to their sons? We do not know. But we do know that rates of infant and child mortality were so high that any less favored child was put at great risk. Although outright infanticide sometimes occurred, death through illness or accident wrought of neglect was more common. To be sure, girls were not the only children at potential risk; so too were disabled or disfigured children, illegitimate children, and unwanted children born into impoverished households. In the case of the Penifader family, only two children are known to have died young, and both were girls.

As young children, Cecilia and her siblings mimicked the gender distinctions that were important to their parents. Coroners' reports show that young boys often died in accidents beyond the house and farmyard; girls most often harmed themselves playing near home. Older boys were killed in mock battles or working in fields or meadows; older girls died by falling into vats or tumbling down wells. Cecilia, staying near the house in the company of her mother, learned how to care for chickens, pigs, cows, and children; how to spin wool into thread; how to cook, brew, and bake; and how to raise the best vegetables and fruits. Her brothers, wandering farther from home in the company of their father, learned how to herd sheep, manage a plow, hunt small game, and cut ripened grains. Yet, although the gender division of labor began

---

[1]In some English towns and also in some regions of the European continent, daughters as well as sons received equal proportions of the inheritance. Even in these cases, however, sons more often took their portions in land and daughters were more likely to take their parts in movable goods.

gaudebunt campi z omnia que in
eis sunt

A harvest scene, with gender roles reversed. In this picture, women are cutting the grain, while the man behind collects it into sheaves. It was more common for men to reap and women to collect, but, as this illustration suggests, the sexual division of labor was not rigid.

at an early age, it was as flexible in childhood as in adulthood. Cecilia might have spent a lot of time around house and farmyard, but like her mother, she also readily worked in pastures and fields. She watched sheep in the pastures; she broke up clumps of earth and weeded in the fields; she bundled and stacked sheaves at harvest.

When Cecilia reached adolescence, differences of gender became more marked. In the years between childhood and adulthood, she was neither completely under the authority of her parents nor entirely free of it. She could attend court, hold land, and work for wages, but she relied heavily on her parents, as many adolescents still do today. She also encountered a variety of new circumstances that differentiated her from her brothers. First, her brothers entered tithings at age twelve. They thereby became part of the peacekeeping community of Brigstock, something that Cecilia and other young women could never do. Second, her brothers were able to get better training and education. Of the few peasants who learned to read and write, all were men. When Cecilia's brother William left Brigstock for school, their parents lost his labor and also perhaps paid some of his expenses; they were willing to make such an investment for a son who might pursue a career as a clerk or priest, but not for a daughter. Of the peasants who learned well-paid skills such as blacksmithing, milling, carpentering, or thatching, all were also men. Women sometimes worked as lower-paid assistants to thatchers or carpenters, but they rarely practiced these trades on their own. Third, Cecilia's brothers were able to get better wages than she could. Whenever the Penifader children worked as day laborers or servants, they found that a man earned much more than a woman. Cecilia earned a penny or less for a day's unskilled work; her brothers got about 1½ pence for similar work. Everyone seemed to accept that, as one contemporary author noted, a woman will work "for much less money than a man would take."

Fourth, parents often not only gave land (rather than goods) to their young sons but also, in so doing, gave them more wealth. This seems to have been true of the Penifaders. Robert and Alice directly gave land to all three of their sons but to only one of their three adult daughters (Christina, probably their eldest girl). Agnes and Cecilia received no lands directly from their parents; both probably got movable goods and cash. In Cecilia's case, her parents might have been "silent partners" in her first small purchases of land, and they almost certainly provided the cash inheritance with which she purchased other properties after their deaths. Cecilia, in other words, was not left impoverished by her parents' arrangements, but she did not get family properties and she probably got less overall than her brothers. Because daughters received less wealth from their parents and less wealth in land itself, landholding in medieval villages was largely a male affair. In Brigstock, about 80 percent of tenants were men.

By the time Cecilia reached her twentieth birthday, she found still further differences between herself and her brothers. Although she was by then an independent tenant in Brigstock, she was barred from a variety of activities, especially pledging and officeholding, that might have enlarged her influence in the community. Her brothers frequently assisted other people in court, standing as pledges to ensure that someone would fulfill a stipulated obligation. All men, poor as well as middling and well-off, could serve as pledges, but women could not. This meant that Cecilia could not help her friends in need, that she could not reciprocate when others pledged for her, and that she could not even make the money that some pledges seem to have gotten for their guarantees. Her brother-in-law Henry Kroyl used pledging to build up a complex network of mutual obligation that involved literally hundreds of people in Brigstock. Cecilia could not do the same. In much the same way, Cecilia could not hold manorial offices, a privilege reserved for males from well-off families. Officeholding could certainly be troublesome, for reeves, jurors, aletasters, and other officers were sometimes fined for dereliction of duty and sometimes attacked by disgruntled neighbors. But officeholding more often than not yielded great advantages—such as the power to control others, the prestige of public authority, and even the profit from fees or gifts. Cecilia's brother Robert served as a juror on several occasions, and her brother-in-law Henry virtually built a career out of public service. Yet, again, Cecilia could not do the same.

These restrictions were born in part of an assumption, apparently little questioned at the time, that women should accept the government of men. "Let not the hen crow before the rooster," as one medieval proverb put it. They were also born of legal traditions that assumed women were less reliable than men, and were, therefore, unacceptable pledges, witnesses, or peacekeepers. Yet these ideas often did not make practical sense. For example, because women could not join tithings, a singlewoman like Cecilia lived outside the peacekeeping mechanisms of the community. Peace would have been better

Animal husbandry. Inside the sheepfold, one person milks while another checks a sheep for illness. Two women carry away pitchers of milk. Dairying was mostly women's work.

ensured by putting Cecilia in a tithing, but this could not be done. Therefore, she lived on Brigstock manor with no father, no husband, and no tithing to take responsibility for her. For another example, women were better qualified than men to supervise the brewing industry; since women brewed the ale, they knew best how to judge its quality, set its prices, and check for cheating. Yet women could not be aletasters. As a result, the ale industry was never as effectively supervised as it might otherwise have been.[2]

Based as they were in often impractical ideas about gender roles, these restrictions affected women's day-to-day life, within the manorial court and without. The court was a center of life in Brigstock. Meeting every three weeks, it was the heart of manor and community, the place where important matters were discussed and important business done. In this central arena of "the community of the vill," women's problems were marginalized. In terms of criminal actions, it seems clear that male violence against women was underreported and lightly treated in medieval courts. In Brigstock, men committed four of every five violent crimes, but suspiciously few of these crimes were assaults on women. Moreover, when women complained of male assaults, their concerns were likely to be dismissed or belittled. For example, women were twice as likely as men to be charged with raising a false hue, needlessly calling their neighbors for help. Some of these women probably misjudged situations or

[2]There are exceptions to the proscription of women from officeholding and pledging in medieval Europe, but they can be counted on a few fingers. On rare occasions, widows temporarily executed the offices of their dead husbands, and widows also, again only rarely, stood as pledges for their children. In both these cases, widows seem to have acquired these special positions not because they were *women* but because they were *heads of households*. Also, in two English communities, a few women have been found listed among the many men who served as aletasters.

even raised hues for malicious and inconsequential reasons. But other women found that their genuine cries for help got them into trouble. In 1302, one woman was even punished for alerting the community to a serious attack. When Matilda Coleman found Adam Swargere hurting her daughter Sarah, she raised a hue against him, and in the View of Frankpledge that October, the incident was reported. Adam's guilt was acknowledged but he was excused from paying any fine; Matilda was forced to pay 7 pence for raising the hue against Adam "unjustly."

In terms of civil actions, women seem to have been similarly disadvantaged, for they used the court to resolve disputes much less often than did men. Women seem to have been less comfortable in court, less familiar with its ways, and less eager to bring problems to its attention. For every four times that a man brought business to court, a woman came once. When a man suffered a trespass on his lands, argued with a neighbor, or sought to settle a bad debt, he took the matter to court. A woman was more likely to settle such matters privately. Cecilia was typical in this regard. In her long life as a householder in Brigstock, she pursued in court only one argument with a neighbor. Her brothers were involved in many more disputes that ended up in court— three for Robert, four for William, and five for Henry.

Cecilia's inability to serve as a pledge or officer shaped her social life as well as her court life. Friendships were based on much more than what happened in the three-weekly meetings of Brigstock's court, but they were extended and strengthened by court activities. For example, thanks to his work as a pledge and an officer, Henry Kroyl was able to do many favors for many people. He was able, in other words, to strengthen dozens of friendships not only by assistance offered in fields and lanes but also by his actions in court. Compared to women (who could not serve as pledges or officers) and poor men (who seldom held office), he was a better neighbor, an important and well-connected man. Because Cecilia could not do the same, her social world was more restricted in size and scope. Like Henry, Cecilia spent most of her time away from the business of the Brigstock court, and she built relationships with people by working with them in the fields, worshipping with them in church, hiring them for a few days' work, walking to markets with them, talking with them over a pot of ale, and otherwise encountering them as she went about her daily business. Like Henry, she also had some social opportunities that were open only to people of her gender. As did other women, she helped at childbirths and celebrated at churchings; as did other men, he marked out the limits of the parish each spring by beating the bounds; and every Sunday, Cecilia stood with the women in the nave, as Henry stood with the men. In many aspects of their daily lives, then, Cecilia and Henry had similar social opportunities—some precisely the same, and some different but not necessarily differently valued. Yet there was one critical difference between them: Cecilia could not use the Brigstock court to expand and enhance her social relationships. As a result, Henry was a more important person in Brigstock. Henry had dozens of strong friends among the people of Stanion and Brigstock. Cecilia relied much more than Henry on a few relationships, especially those based on kin and household.

The gender rules of Brigstock, in short, placed Cecilia at a certain disadvantage. She was born into a world where daughters were less valued than sons. She supported herself in an economy where women earned lower wages than men, got less training for skilled work, and received smaller endowments from their parents. She cooperated with a community structure that proscribed her from participating in its tithings, its pledging networks, and its offices. She relied on a social network that was smaller, narrower, and more focused on nearby neighbors and kin than those of many men. As the daughter of well-off parents, Cecilia forged a prosperous and comfortable life for herself, but she was, all things considered, an exceptionally lucky woman.

GENDER AND HOUSEHOLD

For the Penifader children, then, opportunities divided dramatically according to gender. The Penifader sons knew that they would always enjoy familial, economic, political, and social advantages their sisters lacked. The Penifader daughters knew that they would have a much harder lot in life. To be sure, all was not rosy on one side and horrible on the other. Advantage brought responsibility, as the Penifader boys probably learned at an early age; if they were to inherit family lands, serve in local offices, or become important figures in Brigstock, they had to mature into dutiful and responsible men. Similarly, disadvantage could bring protection, as the Penifader girls might have early discovered. If they were to get less from their parents and have less stature within Brigstock society, they could nevertheless hope that their more favored brothers might watch out for their interests and protect them, if cause arose. The gender rules of medieval villages gave men some powers that women lacked, but they also expected men to use those powers well.

Moreover, the gender rules of medieval villages worked alongside another set of expectations, about householders and their dependents. Men were not just men, and women just women. In theory, each person also had a position in a household: either a head of household or a dependent. In practice, some people were neither heads nor dependents, but they were anomalies in a system that *expected* everyone either to exercise authority within a household or to accept the authority of another. The two systems of gender and household partly complemented one another. The archetypal male, for example, was a married head of household; the archetypal female was a wife. Yet these two systems also sometimes contradicted and confounded one another. For example, as a woman, Cecilia was a lesser member of the community of Brigstock, but as a householder, she took on important public responsibilities. The fault line between householders and dependents often respected distinctions of gender, but when it did not, interesting situations resulted.

The most typical arrangement was exemplified by the conjugal unit, with the husband as head of household and his wife as a dependent under his authority. Legally, a wife lived under **coverture**—that is, she was "covered" in all respects by her husband. For Cecilia's married brother Henry, this circumstance complemented his authority as a male. For her married sisters Christina and Agnes, it complemented their lesser status as females. Women earned less than men, held less land, and had less political and social status, but if they were protected by husbands, these disadvantages could be mitigated. In other words, Agnes, married to the wealthy and powerful Henry Kroyl, enjoyed by proxy his wealth and public authority. Gender and household so complemented each other that when people married, the characteristics ascribed to their gender became, in a sense, heightened: men became more authoritative and more powerful, and women became more dependent and more lacking in power.

The marriage of Agnes Penifader and Henry Kroyl is a good example. Like all young men, Henry was slowly integrated into the public community of Brigstock before he married. He joined a tithing; he acquired land from his parents; he began to attend court and stand as a pledge for others. After he married, he expanded on these roles. He worked more and more as a pledge in court; he began to serve as an aletaster and juror; and he stood before the court as a householder, responsible for the actions of his wife, children, and servants. For Henry, his tentative steps toward adulthood were fulfilled by marriage. The experiences of his wife Agnes were similar, although different in content. She too had taken tentative steps toward adulthood as an adolescent, but like all young women, she encountered some important limitations. She could not join a tithing; she did not receive land from her parents; and she never, as best we can tell, went to the three-weekly meetings of the Brigstock court. After she married, some of the disadvantages that she had known as an unmarried daughter grew stronger. First, as a woman, Agnes always earned low wages, but before marriage, the money was hers to keep or save; after marriage, it belonged to her husband to use as he thought best. Second, Agnes was always less likely than her brothers to acquire land by gift, purchase, or inheritance, but before marriage, such properties (if she could get them) were hers to manage; after marriage, they became part of a conjugal economy controlled by her husband. Third, like many women, Agnes went to court rarely and only if she had to answer specific charges or pleas; after marriage her husband could do even these few things for her. For men, the authority of a married householder was the logical extension of their adolescent powers; for women, the dependency of a married woman was the logical extension of their adolescent disabilities.

Yet, as the Penifader siblings knew well, everybody did not marry, and many wives and husbands ended their lives as widows or, less frequently, widowers. The household circumstances of unmarried adults confounded the neat complementarity of gender and household among married couples. Some singlewomen and bachelors stayed, in terms of their living arrangements, in a state of perpetual adolescence: they lived as servants in the houses of others, lived with parents, or lived alone in hovels. Yet other singlewomen and bachelors were well-off enough to establish their own households: they had their own houses and farmyards; they had their own holdings in fields and pastures; and although they lived without spouses and usually children, they often enjoyed the help and company of servants. Living in this fashion, Cecilia retained throughout her life the stature she had attained by her early twenties. She was an independent tenant and householder, but still a woman. She was more independent than her married sisters (who could not, for example, even sell their lands), but not as authoritative as their husbands (who could, for example, serve in offices). Living in this fashion, Cecilia's brothers William and Robert also retained the stature of their early youth. They were independent tenants and householders, but still not married men. Like other men, they joined tithings and served as pledges, but unlike married men, they could not advance to the most important offices in the community. Robert served twice as a juror, but this was unusual; as a rule, only married men were eligible to serve in manorial offices.

Singlewomen and bachelors sometimes formed atypical households. Because William and Robert produced bastard children, they each might have lived, for a time, with the mothers of these children. If so, their households were illicit, but not unusual; for most purposes, William would have seemed like a husband, and Alice Perse like his wife. Only a visiting bishop might have thought otherwise, and no bishop visited Brigstock during their time. Yet, since an informal union was less stable than a marriage, the lovers of William and Robert were women from relatively poor families. These women might have truly loved William and Robert, but they also might have decided that an informal arrangement with a well-off peasant offered more security than a formal marriage to a poor one. (Love and practical self-interest were not, of course, mutually exclusive.) For poor peasant women, in other words, even an illicit union might have offered some upward mobility.

For Cecilia, only downward mobility would have resulted from bringing a male lover into her household. She would have gained no extra economic security; her family would have objected strenuously; and neighbors would have been scandalized. What could be tolerated for her brothers was not acceptable for her—unless she contracted an upwardly mobile liaison with a

Love. This unskilled drawing touchingly illustrates affection between a woman and a man.

merchant or knight (there is no evidence to suggest that she did). Still, Cecilia did not necessarily end her life ignorant of sexual pleasures. She might have flirted with many men and even made love with some; if so, they would have been wise to restrict their sexual play to activities that would not result in pregnancy. Cecilia, however, almost certainly never brought a man to live with her. Women were another matter. Singlewomen sometimes lived together, and, in at least some of these cases, women who shared homes were lovers, as well as companions and friends. Arrangements such as these are revealed in censuses, letters, and diaries, sources not available for Brigstock in Cecilia's time. But it is certainly possible that Cecilia, like the women revealed in other sources, might have lived with a female companion of some sort, especially during the years that elapsed between the death of her brother William in 1329 and her joint arrangement with Robert in 1336. If so, how did neighbors view a household of two adult women? If the second woman had been Cecilia's servant or lodger, her neighbors would have seen the household as headed by Cecilia. Otherwise, they probably viewed it as a "headless" household composed of two independent adults.

Perhaps the most interesting Penifader household was that created by Robert and Cecilia when they merged their properties in 1336. By the exchanges described in the opening to this chapter, they combined their resources and also their household. For the four years that followed these transactions (Robert died in 1340), brother and sister lived together in one household. Was Robert considered the head of this household? Or were Robert and Cecilia each treated as independent of the other? After this merger, the clerks of the court of Brigstock continued to refer to Robert and Cecilia as separate persons, but on a few occasions they identified Cecilia as "the sister of Robert Penifader." This practice suggests that Cecilia's identity might have become, to some extent, enfolded into the identity of her brother. But even if Cecilia sometimes deferred to her brother and even if their neighbors thought of Robert as the head of their household, Cecilia never fell under the coverture of her brother. Their brother-sister household never fully replicated, in other words, the dynamics of a husband-wife household.

Whereas marriage exacerbated the inequalities of gender and not-married adulthood perpetuated them, widowhood and old age mitigated gender rules. For many men, aging brought less public authority and activity, not more. Few men formally retired, but many slowed down, as did Cecilia's own father during the last years of his life. As he aged, Robert Penifader served less often as an officer of Brigstock, and he also gave more family lands to his children. Many men remained householders throughout their lives, usually remarrying if their wives died, but as their children grew up and departed, they took on fewer responsibilities and fewer obligations. Other men, and women too, even retired from active life, ceding their tenancies to children or others in return for guaranteed support.

For many women, widowhood brought an expansion, rather than a contraction, in public responsibilities. Widows demonstrate clearly how household-status could confound gender-status, since as heads of the households left by their husbands, widows enjoyed certain rights and obligations usually reserved for men. When Cecilia's mother Alice took over the Penifader household after Robert's death, she acquired a host of public opportunities that surpassed those of singlewomen and wives. She could freely trade and sell the lands of the household; she could represent the household and its dependents in court; and, most interesting of all, she could stand as a pledge, if the need arose.[3] Alice did none of these things, for her main public activities after Robert died were to marry off their daughter Agnes and to obtain excuses from attending court. But other widows did what Alice chose not to do; that is, other widows fully exercised their new options as householders. For example, after her husband Peter died in the second year of the Great Famine (1316), Alice Avice changed from a reticent wife into an active widow. She paid the rent on her holding; she purchased some lands and sold others; she answered for several offenses in court; she took six different arguments with neighbors to court; she developed a much wider social network; and she even acted on three occasions as a pledge. Some widows were too old, too withdrawn, or too poor to react to widowhood as did Alice Avice, but all widows had the legal right, as householders, to take on extensive new powers and responsibilities. Toward the end of life, as the powers of old men waned and the powers of widows waxed, differences of gender became less marked.

For the people of Brigstock, then, rules of gender varied with life changes. What it meant to be a woman was different to an adolescent, a wife, a singlewoman, and a widow. What it meant to be a man was different to an adolescent, a husband, a bachelor, and an old man. Most of the rules of gender were built around the ideal of authoritative husbands and dependent wives, but these rules had to adapt to the many people and circumstances that did not fit this ideal. As a woman, Cecilia faced many restrictions on her influence and power; as a householder, she faced many opportunities to enhance her stature. She negotiated a space for herself between the full dependency of married women and the full autonomy of married men.

COMPLICATIONS

It would be a mistake to think that Cecilia was clever to avoid marriage and that her sisters Christina and Agnes were fools to let themselves fall into the dependent status of wives. Things were more complicated than that. Christina and Agnes gained many advantages from marriage: social approval and support; greater economic security; full independence from their parents; and the protection of husbands more publicly powerful than they. They also might have enjoyed many private satisfactions. As they bore children, worked in farmyard and field, brought in money from wage-work, and profited from

[3]Brigstock is unusual in having a few female pledges. Thousands of pledges were offered by men, and only forty-six by women; most involved widows who served as pledges for their children or dependents.

selling foodstuffs, wool, thread, and other items, Christina and Agnes knew they were doing important work. They also knew that wives were so economically essential that most husbands, if left widowed, remarried immediately. As they lived with their husbands in daily intimacy, they might have enjoyed the comfort, affection, and sexual pleasures of a happy relationship. A good marriage could bring a woman many joys and satisfactions. Yes, a wife did not control her own lands or labors, but she could be known as a *goodwife*, respected by her neighbors, appreciated as a wife, and much-loved as a mother.

A bad marriage, however, could be very bad indeed. The gender rules of medieval villages assumed, but did not require, the beneficence of men. If her husband was indifferent or abusive, a woman could find herself a sort of servant to her husband or even cast aside altogether. Some women, such as Margaret Trippes of the diocese of Canterbury, even had to get court orders to force their husbands to provide them with basic support. Other women, such as Margaret Neffield of York whose husband broke her bones and attacked her with daggers and knives, were horribly and repeatedly beaten by their husbands. These sorts of miseries rarely prompted public action, for a husband's rights were extensive, and neighbors were hesitant to intervene. Since divorce was impossible and legal separation was rare, a bad marriage had either to be endured or ended informally (that is, either by desertion or mutual agreement to part ways). As one medieval poem put it, much of a wife's happiness in life depended on her choice of husband:

> The good and bad happenstance that some women have had
> Stands in the choice of good husband or bad.
> For she who a good and faithful husband has found
> Enjoys such a jewel as few who go on ground.
> She who lives with a bad husband in anger and in awe
> In yokes not evenly paired uneasily does draw.

As a singlewoman, Cecilia might have been envied by women in bad marriages, but pitied by those in happy ones. She did not have to worry about an abusive husband or tolerate the restrictions of coverture, but she had to manage without the many advantages of married life. Because she did not marry, her household was poorer than it would otherwise have been, and she missed the possible pleasures of loving children and a loving husband. She was also somewhat odd. In medieval villages, most adults married—so much so that the terms *wife* and *husband* then denoted adults in general, as well as married people in particular. To be sure, there were other singlewomen, bachelors, and widows in Brigstock, some so well-off that they headed their own households and many others who got by as servants, wage-laborers, and lodgers. Rural traditions, however, largely overlooked the lives of these not-married people and praised those whose lives best matched the combined categorizations of gender and household: husbands and wives.

Some peasant women followed a third course, different from the lives of either the singlewoman Cecilia or her married sisters Christina and Agnes. They left their native villages and went to towns, seeking work, shelter, and, perhaps eventually, a good marriage. More women migrated to towns than did men, but it is unclear why. Perhaps women were pushed out of their native villages by the many limitations they faced. After all, they had few opportunities for well-paid work; they were unlikely to hold much land; and their parents, favoring their brothers, might have urged them to move on. Or perhaps they were drawn to the attractions of towns, for towns often *seemed* to offer not only better employment but also better prospects for marriage.[4] So although Cecilia and her sisters stayed close to Brigstock all their lives, they doubtless knew women who, in their late teens or early twenties, left to seek their fortunes in Northampton, Peterborough, or other towns. Wherever they settled, these women had a hard time. They found that the gender rules of medieval towns were strikingly similar to those of Brigstock. Townswomen earned lower wages than men and worked at less skilled jobs; they were usually excluded not only from town government but also from trade gilds; and they were, if married, under the coverture of their husbands. They also found that the life of a new migrant was hard. Much of the available work involved the least desirable and least paid of tasks, such as laundering, spinning, or doing unskilled labor. Although most women migrated in groups or went to towns where they knew a cousin or friend awaited them, they nevertheless sorely missed the broader support of family and kin. Some found themselves so impoverished that they resorted to desperate measures, especially theft and prostitution. Although some women left Brigstock and other manors to seek better fortunes in towns, they were, more often than not, disappointed in what they found.

SUGGESTIONS FOR FURTHER READING

My book on *Women in the Medieval English Countryside: Gender and Household in Brigstock Before the Plague* (1987) elaborates on most of the themes of this chapter. For medieval marriage, see Christopher Brooke, *The Medieval Idea of Marriage* (1989) and R. H. Helmholz, *Marriage Litigation in Medieval England* (1974).

Many recent books have focused on medieval women. The best of these are: Shulamith Shahar, *The Fourth Estate: A History of Women in the Middle Ages* (1983); Margaret Wade Labarge, *A Small Sound of the Trumpet: Women in Medieval Life* (1986); and for England specifically, Henrietta Leyser, *Medieval Women: A Social History of Women in England, 450–1500* (1995). For men, see the essays edited by Clare A. Lees in *Medieval Masculinities, Regarding Men in the Middle Ages* (1994). Two collections of extracts from primary sources are also highly useful: Emilie Amt, *Women's Lives in Medieval Europe: A Sourcebook* (1993), and P. J. P. Goldberg, *Women In England, c. 1275–1525* (1995).

[4]Were the peasant women who migrated to towns "voting with their feet"? Was their migration a form of protest against the difficult circumstances that faced women in the countryside? Perhaps sometimes, but probably not very often. There were no organized protests by medieval women, and it is not at all clear that most women resented their lot in life. But one woman certainly did: in the early fifteenth century, Christine de Pisan published a series of books critical of gender relations in her time. Attached to the French court, de Pisan was an exceptionally privileged and articulate woman, and her ideas make for fascinating reading. See, for example, these modern editions: *The Book of the City of Ladies*, ed. and trans., Earl Jeffrey Richards (1982), and *Treasure of the City of Ladies*, ed. and trans., Sarah Lawson (1985).

CHAPTER 10

Medieval Peasants, Modern People

Cecilia Penifader died in late May or early June, 1344. On 11 June, her kin gathered in the court of Brigstock to argue about her inheritance. Her sister Christina, wife of Richard Power, came from Cranford to claim the inheritance. Her nephew Martin, son of Henry Penifader, asserted a counterclaim. After a jury found that Christina was the nearer kin of Cecilia, she and her husband took possession of the inheritance, and they promptly transferred half of it to Martin. Then a second dispute arose. John, son of William Penifader (Cecilia's nephew), Robert Malin, and Matilda, daughter of Henry Kroyl (her niece) claimed that before Cecilia died, she had leased her lands to them for a term of twenty-four years. Christina and Martin opposed this claim, arguing that Cecilia was mentally incompetent when she made this gift. A second jury was convened, and it determined that although Cecilia had competently arranged the lease, she had never afterwards left her house. Since she had to do so for the lease to take effect, it was deemed invalid.

When Cecilia Penifader was in her mid-forties, she fell sick. For almost a year and a half, she lingered, with her sister, brother-in-law, nephews, and nieces wondering who would be able to claim her many acres of meadow and arable. After her death, the matter came before the Brigstock court. When the court clerk recorded the proceedings that declared Cecilia's lease invalid and designated Christina as the heir of her dead sister's lands, he also idly doodled the figure of a woman in the margins of his court roll. As if dissatisfied with his

Photograph by Peter Moyse, A.R.P.S.

This doodle is located in the margin of a Brigstock court roll that records Cecilia Penifader's death. Notice the clerk's second doodle below the first. This rough drawing might be based on Cecilia Penifader, and, if so, it is the only surviving *portrait* of a medieval peasant women.

first effort (which seems to have produced a woman with two noses), he then redrew the head farther down the margin. Clerks often drew arrows, pointing hands, or other stock images to direct a reader's attention to a particular entry, but they rarely doodled. Perhaps the arguments among Cecilia's kin were so long and protracted that the poor clerk sketched to relieve his boredom. Certainly, he did not draw for love of his skill, as he was not a good artist. Who was the subject of the clerk's drawing on that day in June 1344? Cecilia? Christina? Anywoman? We cannot know, but the possibility that the woman represents Cecilia is intriguing. The clerk would have known Cecilia from her many years of attending court; she was the central figure in the disputes that he recorded in the text adjacent to the doodle; and indeed, he began his sketch immediately next to the line where he began writing, "Cecilia sister of Robert Penifader has died. . . ." If Cecilia is the woman shown in this drawing, we can surmise that she was tall, thin, curly-haired, and perhaps the bearer of a prominent nose. If so, this clerk's doodle provides yet another exceptional artifact about the life of this ordinary woman. Cecilia was just a peasant, but the Brigstock court rolls have revealed a great deal about her family, her life, and now, perhaps even her appearance.

Cecilia's story is exceptional for its documentation, but it must be interpreted with care. To begin with, Cecilia was just one of the millions of peasants who lived in the Middle Ages, and Brigstock was just one of the thousands of villages found in medieval Europe. Not all peasants were like Cecilia, nor were all villages like Brigstock in the early fourteenth century. Moreover, although we can today approach her life with an intimacy that almost seems to close a gap of 700 years, the links between Cecilia's past and our present are not so straightforward. Therefore, we can best put closure on Cecilia Penifader's life by considering how to understand her within the context of medieval history and also within the context of our own time.

CECILIA PENIFADER IN THE MIDDLE AGES

Brigstock, Cecilia's home for more than forty years, was an ordinary sort of medieval community. Nucleated clusters of buildings formed the villages of Brigstock and Stanion; open fields surrounded these houses and farmyards; the products of forest, stream, pasture, meadow, and farmyards supplemented the crops harvested each autumn from the fields; and markets lay within easy reach on any day except Sunday. Yet many other sorts of rural communities dotted the landscape of England and Europe in the Middle Ages. In settlements made on rougher terrain with less fertile soil, peasants organized themselves into smaller hamlets or even isolated farmsteads, and they relied much more on pastoral farming, viticulture, or mining than did the peasants of Brigstock. In villages located near cities, peasants accommodated to urban customers by producing vegetables, grains, or fruits to sell in city markets. In communities near the sea, peasants combined their rural labor with fishing, smuggling, and shipping. All of these variations can be seen within the various regions of Europe; in England, for example, there were shepherds in Yorkshire, tin-miners in Cornwall, market-gardeners in Essex, and fishers on the Devon coast.

These variations, combined with broader patterns of European settlement, climate, soil, and trade, also divided medieval Europe into three general regions. Brigstock lay in the area of classic manorialism, an area that stretched across much of northwestern Europe. To the south, in regions that abutted the Mediterranean, open fields were less common, sharecropping arrangements were often important, and vineyards competed for space with fields of grain. To the east, especially in lands beyond the Elbe that were colonized after 1000, peasants enjoyed better rents and more autonomy than their counterparts to the west, and cultivation of grain predominated over breeding of stock. In short, both within Europe and within its various regions, the medieval countryside was marked by diversity of settlement, social structure, and agrarian practice.

The passage of time brought further diversity. The half-century that encompassed Cecilia's life was a transitional period in medieval history; so much so that some historians place it in the High Middle Ages (usually c. 1000–1350, in their formulations) and others place it within the Later Middle Ages (usually dated, for them, as c. 1300–1500).[1] Their disagreement raises important questions. Should we understand the transformation of medieval civilization as precipitated by the external force of disease, as brought by the Black Death in 1347–49? Or should we consider that the change was internal to Europe, generated by a waning of growth and vitality that began a full fifty years before the plague swept through Europe? For many peasants, the early fourteenth century was certainly a difficult time of overpopulation, low wages, high rents, and the first widespread famine for many centuries. For many landowners, clerics, and merchants, the early fourteenth century was also a troubled era—a time of war between England and France, papal disgrace and relocation to Avignon, monetary crisis, and waning trade. Whether this half-century was the end of one medieval era or the beginning of another, it was certainly a period of trial, uncertainty, and change. As a result, Cecilia's life would have been different if she had been born 100 years earlier or 100 years later. In 1315, Cecilia saw people sicken from hunger during the first year of the Great Famine; in 1215, she would have enjoyed a much greater abundance of food and land; and in 1415, she would have feared plague more than famine. As times changed, so too did distinctions among the regions of Europe. In Cecilia's day, there were many serfs in Western Europe and few to the east; a hundred years later, as serfdom was declining in the West, it was being successfully imposed on the formerly free peasants of Eastern Europe.

These differences of place and time distinguish Cecilia's life as a peasant from the lives of other peasants known to historians: for example, Ermentrude, wife of the peasant Bodo, who lived on an estate outside Paris at the beginning of the ninth century; Mengarde Clergue, the matriarch of a family that dominated the village of Montaillou in southern France at about the time of Cecilia's birth; or even Bertrande de Rols who married Martin Guerre in a village not far from Montaillou some two hundred years after Cecilia died.[2] Because of the

---

[1]For an example ending the High Middle Ages at 1350, see Mortimer Chambers, et al., *The Western Experience* (1998). For an example starting the Later Middle Ages in 1300, see Jackson J. Spielvogel, *Western Civilization* (1997).

[2]For Ermentrude, wife of Bodo, see Eileen Power, *Medieval People* (1924 and many subsequent editions); for Mengarde Clergue, see Emmanuel Le Roy Ladurie, *Montaillou: The Promised Land of Error* (1978); for Bertrande de Rols, see Natalie Zemon Davis, *The Return of Martin Guerre* (1983). Born at the beginning of the sixteenth century, Bertrande de Rols might not seem to qualify as a "medieval" peasant, but she might just make it. Just as historians argue about whether the High Middle Ages had ended by 1300 or 1350, so they also argue about whether the Later Middle Ages should end in 1500 or 1550.

place and time in which she lived, Cecilia was freer of seignorial control than Ermentrude, less tempted by heresy than Mengarde, and not as secure in her landholding as was Bertrande. Throughout the Middle Ages, peasants planted crops, raised sheep, tended vines, and fished streams; throughout the Middle Ages, they worked in social systems, mostly households and communities, that divided their work by age, gender, status, and ability; and throughout the Middle Ages, they owed some of the profit from their work to the Church, some to the manor, and, more often than not, some also to a king. These things were common to medieval peasants, but aside from these, the circumstances of their lives could and did vary widely.

What about Cecilia as a woman, though a woman of peasant status? What might she have shared with other medieval women, particularly those who lived in the towns, manor houses, and castles of early fourteenth-century England? To a surprising extent, gender rules ran across the status lines of medieval England. All women were proscribed from formal political office: countrywomen never worked as reeves, townswomen never served as mayors, and feudal women never sat in parliament. All women also faced similar legal disabilities: inheritance customs preferred sons over daughters whether the property was acreage, shops, or manors, just as courts, whether manorial, mayoral, or royal, treated wives as dependents under the legal authority of their husbands. All women also knew that their public opportunities could wax, wane, and wax again over the life-cycle. They might know some independence as adolescent daughters or adult singlewomen; they could expect to be "wholly within the power" of husbands if married; and they might face the possibility of considerable autonomy as widows. Finally, to some extent, most women did similar work: they bore and reared children; they served as helpmates to their husbands, whether at the plow, in the shop, or on the estate; they prepared food and repaired clothes. Although a knight could not plow and a plowman could not fight on horseback, the wives of such men spun thread with equal ease.

These similarities among medieval women are striking and important, for they suggest that gender rules were strong enough to cut across sharp distinctions of rank and status. Yet these similarities must not obscure the real differences that wealth and status created for medieval women. Cecilia lived in better housing and ate better food than many of her poorer neighbors, but the English aristocrat Elizabeth de Burgh, Lady of Clare, enjoyed a standard of living unimaginable to Cecilia. More importantly, although Cecilia might have punished a wayward servant and offered work to her poorer neighbors, Elizabeth de Burgh exercised an authority over lesser folk—male as well as female—that forever eluded Cecilia. Today, people often talk about how gender is shaped by class, race, and sexuality; for the Middle Ages, it is clear that gender was shaped by birth, wealth, and, as we have seen so clearly for Brigstock, household-status.

In the early fifteenth century, Christine de Pisan, writing from the comforts of the French court, recognized the poverty of peasant women but idealized their status: "Although they be fed with coarse bread, milk, lard, pottage, and water, and although they have cares and labors enough, yet their life is surer—yes, they have greater sufficiency—than some that be of high estate." Christine de Pisan imagined that the arduous lives of peasant women brought them a sort of rugged security lost to aristocratic women. This was an idyllic fantasy, facilitated by de Pisan's own distance from the hard lives of those who actually lived in the cottages of the medieval countryside. Peasant women faced many difficult circumstances, and they did not enjoy any rough and ready equality with their fathers, brothers, and husbands. William Langland, the fourteenth-century English poet who lived in more humble circumstances than Christine de Pisan, offered a much more accurate judgment. In *Piers Plowman*, he wrote of the hunger, the cold, and the work of peasant women, and he concluded "Pitiable it is to read or to show in rhyme the woe of those women who live in cottages!"

CECILIA PENIFADER IN OUR TIME

Interpretation is an essential part of history. Historians spend a lot of time in archives and museums reading old documents, looking at tattered drawings, holding ancient tools and torn clothes. From these sorts of materials, historians are able to verify old facts and uncover new ones, and, in this capacity, they undertake important, and often very satisfying, work. But facts alone do not make history. A fact by itself often means very little. For example, what does it matter that Richard Everard complained in the Brigstock court of August 1316 that Robert Penifader and his daughter Cecilia had taken hay from his land? This is a minor fact about a petty quarrel between unimportant people, and it is a fact that is unlikely to appear in any Western Civilization textbook anytime in the near future. But once interpreted, this fact can reveal interesting things about peasant society—about the tensions that arose from the easily moved boundaries of open fields; about the ways in which petty theft and suspicions between neighbors increased during the Great Famine; even about how fathers could be deemed responsible for the actions of their adolescent children.

Historians interpret at many levels and in many ways. At the microlevel, they ask about the significance of particular facts, such as Richard Everard's complaint against the Penifaders in 1316. At a broader level, they seek to understand past customs and past societies, such as the ways in which medieval peasants sought to manage the lands around their villages. At the most expansive level, historians seek to relate the past to the present. In doing this, three approaches are most common: understanding the past as an antecedent to the present; using it as a tool for understanding human society in general; and examining it as a way to see the present more clearly. These approaches are not mutually exclusive, and each is useful. Weighing changes and continuities, each tries to understand the past not only on its own terms but also in the context of the present. As a result, each can suggest, in the case of Cecilia Penifader, how modern people might best understand the medieval past.

In many respects, Cecilia's world seems radically different from our own. It was, to begin with, more circumscribed. Brigstock manor was large by medieval standards, but small by modern ones; Cecilia spent her life on a manor whose boundaries she could easily walk in one day and among several hundred people whom she knew well. Although other people came and went all the time, Cecilia might have never traveled more than a few dozen miles from Brigstock. Cecilia's world was also much poorer than are the lives of those who live in Brigstock at the turn of the twenty-first century. Cecilia's house was probably one of the best then found in Brigstock, but it was roughly made and furnished with a few simple goods. It had no glazed windows, no chimney, no plumbing. Her diet was healthy and sufficient, but simple and dull. Her clothes were made of rough cloth and simply cut. She also lived within hierarchies that are less accepted today. In early fourteenth-century Brigstock, wives were expected to defer to husbands; peasants to their "social betters"; young to old; poor to better-off. As priests and friars had taught Cecilia, the hierarchy of three orders was God-given and good; some people had more important roles than others, but all people had duties that they should fulfill as best they could. This was, of course, an ideal that everyone did not accept all the time, but for Cecilia the modern notion that all people "are created equal" would have seemed peculiar.

Yet in other respects, there are startling similarities between Brigstock today and Brigstock in the time of Cecilia Penifader. She was, like most people in Brigstock today, raised within the traditions of Christianity; she grew up, as many people do today, in a nuclear family household; she earned, like many women in modern Brigstock, much lower wages than those paid to men; she paid taxes to her central government, as people do today; and although she was not a modern consumer in any sense of the term, she bought many of the goods she required. Cecilia was different from modern people in many ways, but similar in others.

Some historians will interpret Cecilia's story as a precursor to the modern day, a fourteenth-century hint of things that will only be fulfilled in the twenty-first century. In this view, the past becomes the direct ancestor of the present, with a clear and untroubled link between the two. This interpretive approach has appealed to so many historians that it has a long history of its own. In terms of medieval peasants, Alan Macfarlane has been its most ardent proponent.[3] He has suggested that the roots of English individualism and capitalism rest with peasants like Cecilia and villages like Brigstock. Indeed, he would argue that Cecilia was so free of familial constraints and so reliant on markets that she was not really a "peasant" at all. Macfarlane's thesis illustrates how historical interpretation can go awry; his argument is so driven by modern questions (what are the origins of individualism? where did capital-

---

[3]Alan Macfarlane, *The Origins of English Individualism* (1978). This book has been widely criticized by historians. See especially Stephen D. White and Richard T. Vann, "The Invention of English Individualism: Alan Macfarlane and the Modernization of Pre-modern England," *Social History* 8 (1983), pp. 345–363.

ism come from?) that it misunderstands the past. To be sure, Cecilia certainly did rely on markets where she sought to buy some goods and sell others; she also came from a family that readily sold and traded land, without much regard to traditions of familial ownership; and she was able to pick and choose among her kin, favoring some at the expense of others. But Cecilia and other English peasants were not modern before their time. After all, she was a villein of the ancient demesne, subject to the jurisdiction of her manor; she passed her life firmly rooted in the land and the work of her own hands; her social world was profoundly and somewhat narrowly shaped by kinship, community, household, and parish. Cecilia was a well-off peasant who cagily managed her resources, but she was still a peasant, neither a rugged individualist nor an early entrepreneur.

All in all, it is difficult to trace a straight line connecting us back to the fourteenth-century English countryside. First, there have been too many bumps, detours, and changes on the road between Cecilia's world and our own. For example, in the time since Cecilia contributed to the royal taxes of her day, taxation has gone in and out of fashion, its modes of assessment have changed repeatedly (sometimes goods have been taxed, sometimes income, sometimes purchases), and the weight of its burden on ordinary people has gone up and down, again and again. Cecilia paid taxes in the early fourteenth century, and people pay taxes today, but that does not mean that the taxes she paid were a small egg from which have now hatched the huge tax-collecting bureaucracies of our day. Second, it is unlikely that any modern society descends in pristine purity from Cecilia's world. All Western societies today derive in part from the traditions of medieval Europe, but they are built from many other traditions as well. There are no Penifaders in Brigstock today, but if there were, these modern Penifaders would be living in ways shaped by the many histories of people who have lived and died far from Brigstock's borders. When the people of Brigstock today talk with neighbors, dress for work, read newspapers, sit down to supper, play games, and otherwise go about their daily lives, they are part of a broader world economy, world society, and world history. Thanks particularly to modern technologies of transportation and communication, as well as the now-defunct British Empire and the new European Union, life in Brigstock today is immeasurably enriched by the traditions, histories, and customs of many people from many lands. In other words, there are many histories—not a single one going back to Cecilia and her time—that explain the world of Brigstock today, and indeed, the world of all people in the modern West.

Other historians have interpreted the past not as a direct antecedent of the present but instead as a laboratory that can reveal truths about the human condition. This was the intent of George Homans in his 1941 study, *English Villagers of the Thirteenth Century*.[4] The final chapter of this book considered how the history of medieval peasants could illuminate "the elements which societies of different kinds have in common," and, to Homans' mind, his

[4]George C. Homans, *English Villagers of The Thirteenth Century* (1941).

study demonstrated three essential components of any social system (he called these: interaction, sentiment, and function). Today, historians are less willing to generalize so broadly, for we realize that generalization, while useful, can obscure variation and overlook historical context. Yet generalization can be a useful product of history, especially when carefully and hypothetically framed. For example, if women in Brigstock tried to limit their pregnancies with plants and herbs, then it is interesting to consider the possibility that birth control might be used by women of all places and times. The forms might have been cruder and less effective in the past, but perhaps women have always tried to limit their fertility by whatever means they best had. For another example, if people in medieval Brigstock lived, like the people of Brigstock today, in a society fractured by differences between rich and poor, powerful and powerless, then it is useful to wonder if such rankings might be an inevitable part of human life. Cecilia's hierarchies were based primarily on status, wealth, and gender, whereas those today draw on the somewhat different categories of class, race, gender, religion, and world region. But perhaps we share with her the fact of hierarchy, of ranking some people above others. For a final example, if people in Brigstock paid heavy taxes to their king, then perhaps people can always, as the saying goes, trust in two things: death and taxes.

These sorts of parallels between Cecilia's time and our own are striking, and the temptation to draw general conclusions from them is strong. But when generalizing, it is best to seek hypotheses, not conclusions. To begin with, generalizations almost always break down under the weight of numerous exceptions. After all, people in some societies, past as well as present, have not used birth control, have not lived within socioeconomic hierarchies, and have not paid taxes. Moreover, any valid generalizations must be carefully and thoroughly qualified. For example, it is startling that female wageworkers in Cecilia's day earned about the same proportion of a male wage (two-thirds) as do many modern women. Even more startling is that this differential seems to have been roughly maintained for hundreds of years, not only in Europe but also in world regions settled by Europeans. Yet this generalization is not an invariable truth. In some circumstances, wage differentials have either narrowed a bit or expanded a bit, and these changes, however small and temporary, are certainly significant. In addition, in different times and places, wages have been more or less important; in Brigstock today, most people rely on wages or salaries for basic support, but in Cecilia's day, many people supported themselves without ever working for a wage. In Cecilia's day, in other words, wage differentials disadvantaged fewer women than they do today. As this example shows, a valid generalization can be striking and significant, but it must always be understood within the changing and different contexts of societies, past or present.

If some historians interpret the past as precursor and others use the past as a social science laboratory, still other historians see the past as a sort of foreign country. This interpretation is typified by the approach of Henry Stanley

Bennett in his 1937 study, *Life on the English Manor*.[5] Bennett began with a pro-
logue nostalgically titled "A Faire Felde Ful of Folke," and he evoked there the
image of a countryside seen from a hilltop, a land and people that looked to
him both different and familiar. From his distant perch, Bennett sometimes behaved like a stereotypical tourist. At times, he saw medieval peasants as simple folk with odd customs, and at times, he saw their world as impossibly
idyllic, full of harmony and free of conflict. Bennett's particular perspective
would not be adopted by many historians today, for it is too driven by nostal-
gia and too liable to create an exotic and idealized past. But his general approach is still much used, for it offers the critical gift of broader perspective.
For modern people, travel is one popular way to gain perspective. By visiting
new places and meeting new people, we learn to see ourselves on a broader
canvas than before. If we are lucky, we return home from our travels with a
better appreciation of who we are. In a curious twist, therefore, when we
travel, we learn, by appreciating others, to appreciate ourselves as well. History is travel of a different sort, travel in time. It can offer similar rewards.

An interpretation that stresses historical perspective, in other words, en-
courages us to try to understand ourselves through understanding people
who have lived before us. The life and times of Cecilia Penifader offer one
such opportunity. For example, it is interesting to think about our own ideas
of family in light of what *familie* (the Middle English term) meant to Cecilia.
Kin were important to her, but so too were household members, and for most
of her life, she lived in households that included nonkin as well as kin. Moreover, households in Brigstock took on some activities that families rarely do
today. Like us, Cecilia looked for love and emotional support in her household, but she also saw her household as an economic unit—a unit of joint production and consumption. To her, *familie* meant household, and the composi-
tion of her household was fluid and changeable. "Family values," if she could
have understood the term, would have meant taking care of the people with
whom she lived, whether they were kin, servants, or friends. For another example, Cecilia's experience of community should caution against waxing nostalgic about past communities that were, we often seem to imagine, more coherent and unified than our own. Cecilia lived in a small community in which
everyone practiced the same religion, spoke the same language, ate the same
foods, and followed the same customs. Nevertheless, Cecilia's community still
fell short of idyllic harmony: poor peasants resented their well-off neighbors;
newcomers and strangers constantly passed through; and somebody in Brigstock was always guilty of ignoring neighbors' fences, overstocking common
pastures, or taking a bit of grain not their own. Perhaps community is never
complete, always fractured, and always under repair. For a final example, consider how Cecilia was taught that the three orders of her society were divinely
ordained, as was the domination of women by men. Indeed, the medieval

[5]H. S. Bennett, *Life on the English Manor: A Study of Peasant Conditions, 1150–1400* (1937). Unfortunately, I cannot claim any relationship to H. S. Bennett.

Church taught that husbands, in order to discipline their wives, could legitimately beat them. If Cecilia ever questioned these hierarchies of status and gender (and there is no indication that she did), she had to deal with compelling teachings that they were God-given and inevitable. But we do not see things the same way today. To us, the lesson of the three orders can look like a handy justification for the power of the landed elite and wife-beating can look like spousal abuse. What seemed God-given to Cecilia, looks human-made and human-justified today. Or, to put it another way, what looked natural to Cecilia Penifader, looks unnatural to us. How will things that seem natural to us look in a hundred years?

In undertaking this book, I hoped that modern people, through reading about Cecilia's story, might better understand the ordinary lives of medieval peasants—their families, work, communities, superstitions, fears, and hopes. I knew a great deal about the Penifaders and Brigstock when I began, but at every stage of my work, I found myself stumbling across new facts and new possibilities. First, an exceptionally well-educated brother; then, an illegitimate nephew and niece; next, an unusual merging of lands with another brother; by the time I noticed the clerk's doodle in the margin of the court for 11 June 1344, I felt as if Cecilia was demanding, by virtue of the facts appearing before me, that I write her life. In the end, the life of Cecilia Penifader has offered me and, I hope, the readers of this book a detailed story about one medieval peasant and her world. Her story can be understood in different ways, but I hope that those who read her life will remember that she was just one among many medieval peasants and that her life must be historically interpreted, as well as factually known.

Glossary

Note: At their first use in the text, words listed in this glossary are rendered in boldface. Items italicized in this glossary can be found elsewhere in the glossary.

Advowson The right to appoint someone to an ecclesiastical office (such as to be the *rector* of a *parish*). This right of appointment was regarded as a possession that could be passed from one person to another.

Affeeror An officer of the manorial court who determined the amount of fine levied for each reported action or offense.

Aletaster An officer of the *manor* who supervised commercial brewers and *brewsters*. When men and women brewed ale to sell to others, the aletaster was supposed to ensure that ale was well priced, properly measured, and of sufficient quality.

Anchorhold A small cell in which an anchoress or anchorite was voluntarily enclosed to pursue a life devoted to prayer and study. Once sealed into an anchorhold in a special ceremony, the anchoress or anchorite was not ever supposed to come out.

Ancient Demesne Any English *manor* owned directly by William I at the time of the *Domesday Book* survey in 1086. *Villeins* of ancient demesne manors enjoyed special privileges. They did not have to pay tolls or customs anywhere in England, they did not have to attend county courts, and they obtained legal writs from the king. Many ancient demesne manors later passed into nonroyal hands, but the special privileges of the tenants were retained.

Assart Former wasteland, forest, or marsh that had been turned into cultivable land, either surreptitiously or with the permission of the landowner. Assarts were often enclosed by fences or ditches, and they were sometimes called newsets or closes.

Bailiff The chief administrative officer of a *manor*. Typical duties of bailiffs included collecting rents and keeping track of manorial expenses and income. Bailiffs were usually literate men, with a working knowledge of law and business. They supervised *reeves* and *haywards*, who ran manors on a more day-to-day level.

Boon-Work Special labor performed by *serfs* on their manorial *demesnes*. Particularly at times of harvest and haymaking, lords and ladies demanded that serfs work for them for a set number of days, in addition to ordinary *week-work*. Sometimes the entire family was expected to attend boon-works; other times a specified number of adult workers were expected from each household. Often lords and ladies provided food and drink for boon-workers. Although the number of boon-works varied from manor to manor and sometimes from tenant to tenant, they were part of the annual responsibilities of many serfs.

Brewster   A female brewer. Women made most of the ale consumed in medieval England.

By-Laws   Rules applying to the whole community that were agreed on by tenants at manorial courts. By-laws could stipulate, for example, what wages should be paid to harvest-workers or when tenants could release their animals onto *fallow* fields.

Chancel   The sanctuary of a church—that is, the area in which the priest celebrated mass. The chancel was always located to the east of the nave. By tradition, only clergy and their assistants were supposed to go into the chancel, but in practice, men of high social status were often allowed to sit in the chancel during services.

Chevage   Literally, this means an annual payment made by each tenant of a *manor*, but in practice it was usually due only from *serfs* who needed permission to live away from their manors. Serfs who wanted to move to a local town, for instance, might have to pay a few pence a year to compensate their lord or lady for the loss of their labor.

Churching   A religious ceremony, held about six weeks after a birth, that "purified" a new mother and celebrated her successful childbirth. By the Later Middle Ages, churching ceremonies emphasized celebration more than purification, but women were still not allowed to worship in church until after this ritual.

Common Lands   Lands, usually unplanted fields, pastures, or meadows, on which all tenants of a *manor* could graze their animals. *By-laws* often specified how many animals each household could place on these lands.

Coverture   The legal state of wives in medieval England in which they were "covered" by their husbands. Wives under coverture could not sell property or be held responsible for debts; instead, these matters fell under the authority of their husbands.

Cuckingstool   An instrument of punishment usually reserved for women. It consisted of a seat at the end of a pivoting bar. Placed in this seat, the offender would be displayed to her neighbors and often ducked in a pond, ditch, or river. In the early fourteenth century, this punishment was most often applied to *brewsters* who cheated their customers, and it was intended to be humiliating and frightening.

Deacon   A cleric who ranked just below a priest in the hierarchy of religious officials. Deacons often assisted parish priests at their duties, helping at mass, reading scriptures during services, and instructing parishioners. In theory, no one could be ordained a deacon before the age of nineteen.

Demesne   The land on a manor that was not held by tenants but was instead cultivated by *serfs* for the direct profit of the manorial lord or lady. Sometimes, however, the demesne was leased to individual tenants on a short-term basis.

Diocese   The district administered by a bishop and subject to his jurisdiction in matters of Church law. Medieval England was divided into seventeen dioceses and medieval Wales into four. Dioceses were subdivided into other units, of which the most important were *parishes*.

Domesday Book   A survey of English lands, landowners, and tenants commissioned by William I and completed in 1086. Because Domesday Book recorded who owned land and the conditions of their ownership, it was used throughout the Middle Ages as a record of local rights and responsibilities. For example, if Domesday Book recorded that a particular *manor* had been held by the king in 1086, that manor was regarded as part of the *ancient demesne* and its tenants enjoyed special privileges as *villeins* of the ancient demesne.

Dower Lands set aside for a widow to use after her husband's death. Dower lands usually amounted to one-third of the husband's properties. They were often identified by a husband at the time of marriage, but they were also sometimes regulated by custom or law. The remainder of the deceased husband's lands went directly to his heirs. The provision of dower lands for widows was customary among both peasants and members of the elite.

Dowry A payment made by a bride's family to her husband at the time of marriage. Like *dower* lands, dowries were sometimes intended to support wives if their husbands died first. Provision of dowries was most common among members of the elite, and it was more common in southern Europe than in northern Europe. Although forbidden to do so by the Church, many female monasteries also required would-be nuns to offer dowries.

Fallow Unplanted land. Because fertilizers were few and inadequate, medieval peasants let some land lie fallow each year so that, by resting, it could regain its productivity. See also *three-field system* and *two-field system*.

Feudalism The political, military, and social system that maintained the culture and power of the military elite ("those who fight"). The term "feudalism" refers both to the customs of the feudal elite and to the hierarchy among members of this group. Peasants were *not* part of the feudal hierarchy; the lowest-ranking member of the feudal elite was far superior to the highest-ranking peasant. See also chapter 1, footnote 2.

Free Peasant A peasant free of the restrictions and liabilities of *serfs*. Free peasants were allowed to emigrate, work, marry, and take grievances to the king's court. Freedom was determined by birth; if born to parents who were free, a person could claim free status.

Friar A member of one of the mendicant orders founded in the early thirteenth century. The most important of these were the Dominicans and Franciscans. Friars often wandered the countryside, preaching and ministering to the faithful.

Gleaning The practice of going over a harvested field to collect grain that the harvesters had missed. Traditionally, the right to glean was reserved for the young, the old, and the poor.

Hayward Haywards were responsible for the fields of the manor. They often supervised the work of *serfs* at harvest; they ensured that no one stole crops from the *demesne*; they checked that fences were maintained without gaps; and they impounded cattle or sheep that escaped from pastures. Haywards usually served under the direction of reeves.

Heriot A payment made to the manor when an unfree tenant died. Traditionally, the heriot took the form of the *serf's* most valuable animal (the "best beast"), but the surviving members of the household often offered a cash payment instead. See also *mortuary*.

Hue A loud shout made by anyone who came upon the scene of a crime, so that others would help catch the wrong-doer. People who raised the hue without good reason were fined in the manorial court, and people who failed to respond to the hue were also fined.

Jury A panel of six, twelve, or sometimes twenty-four jurors who either reported on misdoings in their community (a "jury of presentment") or judged a case put before them (a "trial jury"). Juries were used at all levels of the English court system, from manorial courts to royal courts.

Leyrwite A payment due to the *manor* from young women of *serf* status, and sometimes young men, if they were found guilty of sex outside marriage.

Manor An estate consisting of land and people. Owned by privileged people or institutions, manors were worked by peasants ("those who work") for the profit of owners. Although one person or institution might own several manors, each manor usually had its own court and own officials.

Manorialism The economic system whereby *serfs* and *free peasants* (who lived on *manors*) supported the landowning elite.

Merchet A payment made to the *manor* when a female *serf* got married.

Mortuary A payment made to the parish priest when someone died. Traditionally, the mortuary took the form of the deceased person's second most valuable animal (the best animal was given to the manor as a *heriot*). This payment was based on the theory that parishioners would be unlikely to have paid all their *tithes* during their lifetimes, so the mortuary compensated for tithes unpaid. In some places mortuaries were charged on all deaths, wives and children included, while in other places they applied only to male householders.

Nave The main area of a church, where the congregation gathered to hear services. The nave stretched between the *chancel* at the east end, where the priest celebrated mass, and the bell tower at the west end. Through most of the Middle Ages, naves did not contain pews, so people attending church stood, squatted, or sat on the floor. The upkeep of the nave was the responsibility of the parishioners.

Oblation A payment made to a priest in return for his services in baptizing, marrying, burying, or otherwise caring for the soul of an individual parishioner. In theory, the payment was voluntary, but it was customary and expected.

Open Fields Fields surrounding medieval villages in which many tenants held separate *strips* of land for growing crops. Because an open field was not divided by fences, only boundary stones or other markers separated the strips of various tenants. While open fields enabled easy plowing and planting, they were the subject of conflict in manorial courts; peasants often complained that boundaries had been moved or that their neighbors had taken grain from the wrong strip.

Parish The smallest geographical unit in the ecclesiastical system. In the early fourteenth century, England and Wales contained about 9,000 parishes, each under the religious authority of a parish priest and his assistants. For most ordinary people, parishes were the focus of worship and religious activity.

Parish Clerk A man hired to assist a parish priest at his duties, especially the reading and writing of documents.

Parson Any priest responsible for a parish, whether a *rector* or *vicar*.

Pence The plural of penny, the basic medieval coin. Twelve pence made a *shilling;* 240 pence made a *pound sterling*. In the fourteenth century, female laborers usually earned 1 penny or less for each day's work, whereas a male laborer got about 1½ pence. In documents, pence were abbreviated as d., short for the Latin word *denarius*.

Pledge In the context of a manorial court, a person who guaranteed that another person would pay a stipulated fine or perform a specified obligation. If the fine remained unpaid or the obligation unfulfilled, the pledge was liable. Pledges were almost always men, and often they were men of high social standing on the *manor*.

Pound Sterling A monetary unit worth 240 pence or 20 shillings. The symbol for a pound sterling is £, which derives from the Latin word *libra*.

Rector A priest or institution appointed to attend to the religious needs of members of a *parish*. Many rectors directly served their parishes as priests, but some lived away from their parishes and paid *vicars* to do their work for them. In Brigstock, the rector of the parish was an institution, the Abbey of Circencester. As a result, it was always necessary to appoint a vicar to do the day-to-day work of serving as parish priest of Brigstock.

Reeve After the *bailiff*, the most important officer on a *manor*. Reeves managed much of the daily business of the manor, such as making sure that the *demesne* lands were properly plowed, sown, and harvested, and that rents of leased portions of the demesne were duly paid. The reeve supervised the *hayward*.

Rod A small measurement of land. The exact area encompassed by a rod varied slightly from place to place. In Brigstock, four rods made an acre.

Serf An unfree peasant. Serfs were not allowed to move around from place to place; rather they were regarded as being attached to the land. Serfs were expected to work for the *manor* on a weekly basis (see *week-work*) and at special times of the year (see *boon-work*). They also had to pay various fines and fees to their manor on particular occasions (see *chevage, heriot, merchet, tallage*). Serfdom was determined by birth. If born to parents who were serfs, a person inherited the status of serf. In England, serfs were called *villeins*.

Shilling In the medieval monetary system, 12 *pence*. Twenty shillings made a *pound sterling*. In documents, a shilling was abbreviated as s., short for the Latin word *solidus*.

Singlewoman The medieval term for a woman who never married. In the Middle Ages, the term "spinster" described a woman who worked at spinning wool into thread.

Stocks Instruments of punishment in which the offender's feet or hands were tied or locked into a wooden frame. The offender was left on display in this position for a specified length of time. Millers and bakers who cheated their customers were particularly likely to be punished in this way. Stocks were employed as a mode of punishment by English colonists in North America, and surviving examples can often be seen at historic villages or museums.

Strip A long narrow area of land within an *open field* in which crops were grown. Strips were of varying widths and were demarcated by stones or other markers, not fences. Each family might hold one or more strips in several fields surrounding a village.

Tallage A tax on *serfs* that could be levied at will by manorial lords or ladies. Sometimes tallage was assessed according to the amount of land or the number of animals a tenant held; on other occasions a set amount was charged per individual; and on still other occasions, tenants as a group were charged a particular amount and left to work out among themselves how best to divide the expense.

Three-Field System A system of farming in which peasants rotated crops each year between three fields: the first field grew a winter crop such as wheat; the second grew a spring crop such as barley; and the third was unplanted (it lay *fallow*) to replenish the soil. The next year, the first field grew a spring crop, the second lay fallow, and the third was sown with a winter crop. The three-field system was an innovation of the High Middle Ages, an improvement on the *two-field system*.

Three Orders   An idea, created and promoted by the medieval clergy, that society was composed of three interdependent and ranked groups: first, "those who pray" (priests, monks, nuns, bishops, and other religious professionals); second, "those who fight" (knights, ladies, and other members of the landowning classes); and last, "those who work" (peasants).

Tithe   An obligatory payment to the Church of 10 percent of all profits and produce. All members of society, from the wealthiest aristocrats to the poorest peasants, were expected to pay tithes.

Tithing   A group of men (originally, ten men) responsible for the behavior of each member. If a member of a tithing was accused of committing a crime, the other members of the tithing had to ensure that he was brought before the manorial court for judgment. If they failed to produce their accused member, the entire tithing could be liable for punishment. Male peasants were sworn into tithings at the age of twelve.

Tithingman   The man in charge of a *tithing*. Tithingmen were elected annually and were often expected to serve on *juries* in manorial courts.

Two-Field System   A system of farming in which peasants rotated crops each year between two fields: one field was planted with crops while the other was unplanted (it lay *fallow*) to replenish the soil. The next year, the planted field lay fallow while the fallow field was planted. In the eleventh century, many villages began to switch to the more efficient *three-field system*.

Vicar   A priest who stood in for an absent *rector* in doing the day-to-day work of looking after the religious needs of people in a *parish*.

View of Frankpledge   A special court convened twice a year (or sometimes once a year, as in Brigstock) to make sure that every male over the age of twelve was enrolled in a *tithing* and to punish people guilty of crimes and petty offenses.

Village   A cluster of peasant houses. Villages varied considerably in size, from small hamlets of only a few households to settlements of several hundred people. The boundaries of *manors* and *parishes* were not always the same as those of villages.

Villein   The English term for *serf*.

Week-Work   The obligation of some *serfs* to work for a few days each week on the manorial *demesne*. Typical duties included plowing, sowing seed, mending farm buildings, carting dung, harvesting grain, and caring for animals. Serfs performing week-work were supervised by the *reeve*.

Index

Photo Credits

Chapter 1, (p. 2): Sloane 2453, fol. 85 © The British Library, London

Chapter 2, (p. 18): MS. CCC 285, fol. 3v © Corpus Christi College, Oxford, UK/Bridgeman Art Library, London/New York

Chapter 3, (p. 32): MS. Roy.2.B.vii, fol. 78v © The British Library, London

Chapter 3, (p. 33): Add 42130 (Luttrell Psalter), fol. 173v © The British Library, London

Chapter 4, (p. 52): IND41446 A tutor with his pupils by Fra Antoni Canals, 14–15th century. Archivo Municipal, Barcelona, Spain/Index/Bridgeman Art Library, London/New York

Chapter 4, (p. 56): MS. Douce 5, fol. 2r © Bodleian Library, Oxford, U.K.

Chapter 4, (p. 58): Stowe 17, fol. 38 © The British Library, London

Chapter 5, (p. 63): MS. Selden Supra 38, fol. 21v © Bodleian Library, Oxford, U.K.

Chapter 5, (p. 69): Add 42130 (Luttrell Psalter), fol. 196v © British Library, London, UK/Bridgeman Art Library, London/New York

Chapter 5, (p. 71): MS. B.11.22, fol. 55v © Cambridge University Library, U.K.

Chapter 6, (p. 75): MS. Douce 6, fol. 22r © Bodleian Library, Oxford, U.K.

Chapter 6, (p. 76): MS. 24, fol. 34 © The Pierpont Morgan Library/Art Resource, NY

Chapter 6, (p. 83): MS. e. Mus. 60, fol. 78r © Bodleian Library, Oxford, U.K.

Chapter 7, (p. 89): Add 42130 (Luttrell Psalter), fol. 166v © British Library, London, UK/Bridgeman Art Library, London/New York

Chapter 7, (p. 92): Add 42130 (Luttrell Psalter), fol. 74v © The British Library, London

Chapter 7, (p. 93): Add 42130 (Luttrell Psalter), fol. 170 © British Library, London, UK/Bridgeman Art Library, London/New York

Chapter 7, (p. 95): MS. B.11.22, fol. 160v © Cambridge University Library, U.K.

Chapter 8, (p. 104): Add 42130 (Luttrell Psalter), fol. 173 © British Library, London, UK/Bridgeman Art Library, London/New York

Chapter 8, (p. 109): MS. Douce 5, fol. 29r © Bodleian Library, Oxford, U.K.

Chapter 9, (p. 117): Add 42130 (Luttrell Psalter), fol. 172v © British Library, London, UK/Bridgeman Art Library, London/New York

Chapter 9, (p. 119): Add 42130 (Luttrell Psalter), fol. 163v © British Library, London, UK/Bridgeman Art Library, London/New York

Chapter 9, (p. 123): MS. Rawl. D. 939, section 3 © Bodleian Library, Oxford, U.K.